THE AUSTRALIAN
Women's Weekly

simple shortcuts

Let these supermarket time-savers deliver stress-free meals

BAUER

MEDIA GROUP

CONTENTS

HOME-COOKED HELP

In our busy lives it's hard to find time for the little things, but it's often the little things we miss most. Enjoying a home-cooked meal is one of life's simple pleasures and something that doesn't have to be difficult or complicated. With a few clever tricks, you can avoid the stress of getting dinner on the table every night.

THE EQUIPMENT

Take a look through your kitchen cupboards. Is there a food processor hiding in the corner? Were you given a good set of knives, a V-slicer or a mortar and pestle as a wedding present? Knowing what equipment you have at your disposal will prompt you to use it to make life easier in the kitchen. Store your equipment somewhere easily accessible and make sure everything is in good condition. All blades including knives, vegetable peelers and graters should be kept sharp. Don't underestimate how common kitchen gadgets like blenders and processors can help speed up the meal preparation process. Even the humble microwave can reduce cooking times; use it to defrost meat, melt butter or steam vegies.

THE PANTRY

Once your kitchen is arranged logically, take time each weekend to make a weekly meal plan. Choose the meals for the week and read through each recipe so you know what you're in for. Make a shopping list of all the ingredients you'll need and you'll quickly discover items that appear repeatedly – these can be kept as pantry staples. Buy oil, vinegar, salt, sugar, flour, pasta, rice, herbs and spices in advance, then you'll only need to get fresh produce each week. When you have the essentials readily on hand you'll be less likely to give up and order takeaway. And with these tips, you'll have dinner ready sooner than your order would arrive.

THE SUPERMARKET

When you pay a visit to your local supermarket to stock up on items for your pantry, you'll be hard pressed not to notice the wide array of pre-packaged products on offer. As well as canned goods and frozen vegetables, quality products including salad mixes, pre-cut and peeled vegetables, stir-fry mixes, pizza bases, frozen pastry and barbecued chickens will make life easier by cutting down on preparation time. Similar savings are found at the butcher, where you can buy from a range of trimmed, sliced, diced, marinated, crumbed and skewered meats. You can also make recipes faster by replacing home-made pasta sauces, curry pastes, marinades and salad dressings with store-bought versions.

THE FRIDGE

Once you've purchased your ingredients, take the opportunity to save even more time by marinating meat in the fridge overnight. Anything that can be done ahead of time will be rewarded when you come home to find dinner already prepped in the fridge. When it's time to cook, just be sure to anticipate the recipe's steps by preheating the oven, boiling the kettle and weighing and measuring everything before you begin.

THE FREEZER

Go one step further and make double of a recipe one night and freeze the leftovers for another night, or take advantage of your weekends by cooking meals in batches for the busy week ahead. There's nothing quicker than reheating leftovers, and they can be just as good for lunch the next day.

Alternatively, there are a number of features throughout this book where we use a base recipe to create two or more recipes. In this instance, you can increase the base recipe and either refrigerate or freeze the extra servings, depending on how soon you plan to use them. Make sure that you label and date anything going into the freezer so you can find what you're looking for when you're in a rush.

THE KITCHEN

Cooking good food doesn't have to be a chore. It can even be done quickly with the right equipment, some organisation and a little bit of confidence. Cook at home with these shortcuts, and you'll not only save time and money, you'll also discover how to make the most of your kitchen.

CHICKEN

chicken salad

PREP TIME 35 MINUTES SERVES 4

1 long french bread stick, sliced thinly

2 tablespoons olive oil

3 cups (480g) shredded barbecue chicken

4 stalks celery (600g), trimmed, sliced thinly

1 medium white onion (150g), chopped finely

3 large dill pickles (150g), sliced thinly

2 tablespoons finely chopped fresh flat-leaf parsley

1 tablespoon finely chopped fresh tarragon

1 large butter (boston) lettuce, leaves separated

⅔ cup (160ml) creamy ranch dressing

1 Brush both sides of bread slices with oil; toast under preheated grill (broiler) until browned lightly both sides.

2 Combine chicken, celery, onion, pickle and herbs in a large bowl; toss gently.

3 Place lettuce leaves on a serving platter; top with salad and toast slices, drizzle with dressing and a little extra olive oil, if you like.

Green curry is traditionally the hottest-flavoured Thai curry – if you find it too hot, add a little extra coconut cream or chicken stock to reduce the heat.

green curry with chicken meatballs

PREP + COOK TIME 40 MINUTES **SERVES** 4

2 tablespoons peanut oil

800g (1½ pounds) prepared chicken meatballs

¼ cup (75g) green curry paste

3¼ cups (810ml) coconut cream

2 tablespoons fish sauce

2 tablespoons lime juice

1 tablespoon grated palm sugar

150g (4½ ounces) sugar snap peas, trimmed

1 cup (80g) bean sprouts

⅓ cup loosely packed fresh coriander leaves (cilantro)

⅔ cup (100g) roasted unsalted cashews

1 fresh long green chilli, sliced thinly

lime wedges, to serve

1 Heat half the oil in a large frying pan over high heat; cook chicken balls until browned.
2 Meanwhile, heat remaining oil in a large saucepan over medium-high heat; cook paste, stirring, for 2 minutes or until fragrant. Add coconut cream, sauce, juice and sugar; bring to the boil. Reduce heat; simmer, uncovered, for 20 minutes. Add meatballs to the pan; stir in peas. Simmer, uncovered, until meatballs are cooked through and peas are tender.
3 Serve curry sprinkled with sprouts, coriander leaves, nuts and chilli; accompany with wedges.

SERVING SUGGESTION Steamed jasmine rice or rice noodles.

TIP Prepared chicken meatballs are available from most major supermarkets, chicken shops and butcher shops; if you can't find them, roll chicken patties into balls. Some store-bought meatballs are par-cooked; there is no need to brown these.

nutritional count per serving
- ▶ 80.5g total fat
- ▶ 44.7g saturated fat
- ▶ 4243kJ (1015 cal)
- ▶ 19.7g carbohydrate
- ▶ 50.6g protein
- ▶ 9.1g fibre

nutritional count per serving
▶ 19.3g total fat
▶ 3.6g saturated fat
▶ 1822kJ (436 cal)
▶ 29.2g carbohydrate
▶ 34.3g protein
▶ 4.4g fibre

fried chicken with cabbage

PREP + COOK TIME 20 MINUTES **SERVES** 4

400g (12½ ounces) frozen tempura chicken pieces

1 tablespoon peanut oil

3 green onions (scallions), sliced thinly

2 cloves garlic, crushed

600g (1¼-pound) packet shredded coleslaw mix

¼ cup (55g) caster (superfine) sugar

¼ cup (60ml) chinese black vinegar

2 tablespoons light soy sauce

1 Cook chicken following packet directions.

2 Heat oil in a wok over high heat; stir-fry onion and garlic until fragrant. Return chicken to wok with remaining ingredients; stir-fry until heated through, season to taste.

TIP Frozen tempura chicken is available from major supermarkets and Asian grocery stores. You can make your own tempura chicken using a store-bought tempura batter mix. For best results, cut 400g (12½ ounces) of chicken breast fillets into serving size pieces; dry with kitchen paper, then coat with the batter. Deep-fry the chicken in batches until golden brown.

test kitchen tip

Chinese black vinegar is a dark-coloured vinegar with a smoky, malt flavour that works well in stir-fries, braises and marinades. It is available from Asian grocery stores and some larger supermarkets.

chicken, zucchini and mushroom lasagne

PREP + COOK TIME 1¼ HOURS SERVES 6

⅓ cup (80ml) olive oil

1 medium brown onion (150g), chopped finely

2 cloves garlic, crushed

500g (1 pound) minced (ground) chicken

2 tablespoons tomato paste

410g (13 ounces) canned diced tomatoes

1 teaspoon caster (superfine) sugar

⅓ cup coarsely chopped fresh basil

3 medium zucchini (360g), sliced thinly

5 flat mushrooms (400g), sliced thinly

400g (12½ ounces) ricotta

½ cup (125ml) milk

1 egg, beaten lightly

375g (12 ounces) fresh lasagne sheets

⅓ cup (25g) finely grated parmesan

1 Preheat oven to 200°C/400°F.

2 Heat 1 tablespoon of the oil in a medium saucepan; cook onion and garlic, stirring, until onion softens. Add chicken; stir until browned. Add paste, tomatoes and sugar; bring to the boil. Reduce heat; simmer, uncovered, for 5 minutes. Stir in basil; season.

3 Cook zucchini and mushrooms, in batches, on a heated oiled grill plate (or grill or barbecue), brushing with remaining oil, until browned and tender.

4 Meanwhile, combine ricotta, milk and egg in a medium bowl.

5 Line the base of a 2-litre (8-cup) ovenproof dish with lasagne sheets, trimming to fit. Top with one-third of the chicken mixture, half the vegetable mixture and half the ricotta mixture. Top with lasagne sheets, trimming to fit. Top with half the remaining chicken mixture, remaining vegetable mixture, lasagne sheets, then remaining chicken mixture. Top with remaining lasagne sheets and remaining ricotta mixture; sprinkle with parmesan.

6 Cover dish with foil; bake for 20 minutes. Uncover dish; bake for about 30 minutes or until browned lightly. Stand for 10 minutes before serving.

SERVING SUGGESTION Mixed green salad.

TIP You can replace the ricotta mixture with a store-bought béchamel or cheesy white sauce.

nutritional count per serving
▶ 34.8g total fat
▶ 13.4g saturated fat
▶ 2909kJ (696 cal)
▶ 59.8g carbohydrate
▶ 34.4g protein
▶ 6.6g fibre

satay chicken

satay chicken

PREP + COOK TIME 20 MINUTES **SERVES** 4

2 tablespoons peanut oil

750g (1½ pounds) chicken breast stir-fry strips

200g (6½-ounce) packet satay sauce

1 large carrot (180g), cut into matchsticks

¼ cup (35g) coarsely chopped roasted unsalted peanuts

2 green onions (scallions), sliced thinly

1 Heat oil in a wok over high heat; stir-fry chicken, in batches, until browned.
2 Add sauce and carrot to wok; stir-fry until chicken is cooked and carrot is tender. Remove from heat; season.
3 Serve the satay sprinkled with nuts and onion.

SERVING SUGGESTION Steamed jasmine rice.

TIP Rather than chopping the nuts, use crushed or granulated peanuts.

chicken and sweet corn bake

PREP + COOK TIME 25 MINUTES **SERVES** 4

3 cups (480g) coarsely chopped barbecued chicken

420g (13½ ounces) canned creamed corn

1½ cups (180g) coarsely grated cheddar

½ cup (125ml) pouring cream

4 green onions (scallions), sliced thinly

1 cup (70g) stale breadcrumbs

1 Preheat oven to 220°C/425°F.
2 Combine chicken, corn, cheese, cream and onion in a large bowl; season. Spoon mixture into four oiled 1-cup (250ml) ovenproof dishes; sprinkle with breadcrumbs.
3 Place dishes on an oven tray; bake for about 20 minutes or until mixture is heated through and the top is browned lightly.

SERVING SUGGESTION Mixed green salad.

TIP You need to purchase a large barbecued chicken to get the amount of shredded meat required for this recipe.

(photograph page 16)

nutritional count per serving
▶ 49.6g total fat
▶ 22.4g carbohydrate
▶ 17.7g saturated fat
▶ 66.4g protein
▶ 3377kJ (808 cal)
▶ 6.6g fibre

nutritional count per serving
▶ 26.9g total fat
▶ 27.2g carbohydrate
▶ 14.4g saturated fat
▶ 30.4g protein
▶ 2006kJ (480 cal)
▶ 5.1g fibre

chicken and sweet corn bake (see recipe page 15)

test kitchen tip

Tandoori paste is a paste
of medium heat and includes
coriander, garlic, tamarind,
ginger, chilli and other spices,
which are used to give foods
the authentic red-orange tint
of tandoor oven cooking.

tandoori chicken (see recipe page 18)

tandoori chicken

PREP + COOK TIME 25 MINUTES **SERVES** 4

1 cup (280g) low-fat plain yoghurt

⅓ cup (100g) tandoori paste

4 chicken breast fillets (800g)

TOMATO AND CORIANDER SALSA

170g (5½-ounce) punnet grape tomatoes, sliced thinly

1 small red onion (100g), chopped finely

2 teaspoons caster (superfine) sugar

2 tablespoons finely chopped fresh coriander (cilantro)

1 Combine yoghurt and paste in a large bowl. Add chicken; turn to coat in marinade.
2 Cook chicken on a heated oiled grill plate (or grill or barbecue), brushing with marinade, until browned both sides and tender.
3 Meanwhile, make tomato and coriander salsa.
4 Slice chicken thickly; serve with salsa.

TOMATO AND CORIANDER SALSA Combine ingredients in a small bowl.

SERVING SUGGESTION Steamed or microwaved basmati rice and pappadums.

(photograph page 17)

nutritional count per serving	
▶ 12.3g total fat	▶ 11.1g carbohydrate
▶ 4.2g saturated fat	▶ 47.3g protein
▶ 1467kJ (351 cal)	▶ 1.1g fibre

chilli chicken stir-fry

PREP + COOK TIME 20 MINUTES **SERVES** 4

2½ cups (500g) jasmine rice

1 tablespoon sesame oil

800g (1½ pounds) chicken stir-fry strips

⅓ cup (100g) thai chilli jam

2 tablespoons sweet chilli sauce

¼ cup (60ml) chicken stock

225g (7 ounces) canned sliced water chestnuts, rinsed, drained

400g (12½-ounce) packet fresh or frozen stir-fry vegetable mix

1 tablespoon sesame seeds, toasted

1 Cook rice in a large saucepan of boiling water until just tender; drain. Cover to keep warm.
2 Meanwhile, heat half the oil in a wok; stir-fry chicken, in batches, until cooked through. Return chicken to wok with jam, sauce and stock; stir-fry for about 2 minutes or until sauce thickens slightly. Remove from wok.
3 Heat remaining oil in same cleaned wok; stir-fry water chestnuts and vegetable mixture until just tender and heated through.
4 To serve, top vegetable mixture with chilli chicken, sprinkle with sesame seeds; accompany with rice.

TIPS Use microwave rice instead of cooking your own to save time. Replace vegetable mixture with 500g (1 pound) baby buk choy and 1 thinly sliced large red capsicum (bell pepper).

nutritional count per serving	
▶ 13.7g total fat	▶ 115.9g carbohydrate
▶ 2.7g saturated fat	▶ 57.6g protein
▶ 3490kJ (835 cal)	▶ 5.4g fibre

chilli chicken stir-fry

fettuccine alla pizzaiola

PREP + COOK TIME 35 MINUTES **SERVES** 4

2 tablespoons olive oil

4 crumbed chicken breast schnitzels

7 slices prosciutto (110g)

3 cups (780g) olive and tomato pasta sauce

1¾ cups (175g) grated mozzarella

250g (8 ounces) fettuccine

TIPS Fettuccine comes from the Italian word 'fettucina', meaning ribbon, because of its long, narrow shape. It goes especially well with creamy sauces; you can replace it with tagliatelle or other large egg noodles, if desired. Fresh pasta cooks even faster than dried pasta; you can find fresh pasta in most supermarkets in the refrigerated section.

1 Preheat oven to 200°C/400°F.

2 Heat oil in a large frying pan; cook chicken, in batches, until browned lightly.

3 Place chicken, in a single layer, in a medium shallow baking dish; top with prosciutto, sauce then cheese. Cook, uncovered, in oven, for about 20 minutes or until chicken is cooked through.

4 Meanwhile, cook pasta in a large saucepan of boiling water until just tender; drain. Serve pasta topped with chicken pizzaiola.

nutritional count per serving
- ▶ 42.4g total fat
- ▶ 13g saturated fat
- ▶ 3821kJ (914 cal)
- ▶ 72g carbohydrate
- ▶ 52.9g protein
- ▶ 6.1g fibre

chicken pie with cheesy mash

PREP + COOK TIME 50 MINUTES **SERVES** 6

2 teaspoons vegetable oil

1 medium brown onion (150g), chopped finely

750g (1½ pounds) minced (ground) chicken

1 medium carrot (120g), chopped finely

2 stalks celery (300g), trimmed, chopped finely

¼ cup (35g) plain (all-purpose) flour

1 cup (250ml) chicken stock

2 tablespoons worcestershire sauce

155g (5 ounces) button mushrooms, quartered

¾ cup (120g) frozen peas

2 x 600g (1¼-pound) tubs prepared mashed potato

½ cup (40g) finely grated parmesan

1 Preheat oven to 200°C/400°F.

2 Meanwhile, heat oil in a large saucepan over medium-high heat, add onion and chicken; cook, stirring, until browned. Add carrot and celery; cook, stirring, until soft. Stir in flour then gradually add stock, sauce and mushrooms; cook, stirring, until mixture boils and thickens. Stir in peas; season.

3 Spoon mixture into a 2.5-litre (10-cup) ovenproof dish; top with mash, sprinkle with parmesan.

4 Bake pie, uncovered, for about 30 minutes or until browned and heated through.

SERVING SUGGESTION Green leaf and tomato salad.

TIPS This pie is suitable to freeze. Thaw in the fridge overnight before reheating.
You can replace the carrots, celery, mushrooms and peas with a 400g (12½-ounce) packet of fresh diced vegetable soup mixture – this is found in the vegetable or refrigerated sections of most larger supermarkets, as well as many greengrocers.

nutritional count per serving
- 31.7g total fat
- 13.5g saturated fat
- 2976kJ (712 cal)
- 49g carbohydrate
- 52.4g protein
- 10.6g fibre

LAMB

lamb kofta with spicy tomato chutney

PREP + COOK TIME 20 MINUTES SERVES 6

1kg (2 pounds) minced (ground) lamb

1 large brown onion (200g), chopped finely

1 clove garlic, crushed

1 tablespoon ground cumin

2 teaspoons allspice

2 teaspoons ground turmeric

1 tablespoon finely chopped fresh mint

2 tablespoons finely chopped fresh flat-leaf parsley

1 egg, beaten lightly

6 pitta pocket breads (510g), quartered

200g (6½-ounce) tub tzatziki

½ cup (160g) spicy tomato chutney

1 Combine lamb, onion, garlic, spices, herbs and egg in a large bowl. Divide mixture into 18 even-sized pieces; mould around skewers to form sausage shapes.
2 Cook kofta, in batches, on a heated oiled grill plate (or grill or barbecue) until cooked through.
3 Serve kofta with pitta, tzatziki and chutney.

SERVING SUGGESTION Tabbouleh or a greek salad.

TIPS If using bamboo skewers, soak in water for at least 30 minutes to prevent them scorching during cooking, or cover the ends with foil.
For a simple tzatziki sauce, combine ¾ cup low-fat yoghurt, 1 clove crushed garlic and 1 tablespoon finely chopped fresh flat-leaf parsley in a small bowl.
For a simple chilli tomato sauce, combine ¼ cup tomato sauce (ketchup) and ¼ cup chilli sauce in a small bowl.

nutritional count per serving
▶ 14.1g total fat
▶ 5.7g saturated fat
▶ 1931kJ (462 cal)
▶ 38.2g carbohydrate
▶ 43.2g protein
▶ 3.1g fibre

3 WAYS WITH MEAT SAUCE

pastitsio

PREP + COOK TIME 1¾ HOURS SERVES 6

400g (12½ ounces) fresh ricotta

½ cup (40g) finely grated parmesan

1 egg, beaten lightly

250g (8 ounces) macaroni

2 eggs, beaten lightly, extra

¾ cup (60g) coarsely grated provolone cheese

2 tablespoons fresh breadcrumbs

MEAT SAUCE

2 tablespoons olive oil

2 medium brown onions (300g), chopped finely

800g (1½ pounds) minced (ground) lamb

410g (13 ounces) canned crushed tomatoes

⅓ cup (90g) tomato paste

½ cup (125ml) beef stock

⅓ cup (80ml) dry white wine

½ teaspoon ground cinnamon

1 egg, beaten lightly

1 Make meat sauce.

2 Meanwhile, combine ricotta, parmesan and egg in a medium bowl. Refrigerate until required.

3 Preheat oven to 180°C/350°F. Oil a shallow 2.5-litre (10-cup) ovenproof dish.

4 Cook pasta in a large saucepan of boiling water until tender; drain. Combine hot pasta, extra beaten eggs and provolone in a large bowl. Press pasta mixture over base of dish.

5 Top pasta evenly with meat sauce; spoon over ricotta mixture, then sprinkle with breadcrumbs.
6 Bake pastitsio about 1 hour or until browned lightly. Stand for 10 minutes before serving.

MEAT SAUCE Heat oil in a large saucepan over medium-high heat; cook onion and lamb, stirring, until lamb is browned. Stir in tomato, paste, stock, wine and cinnamon; simmer, uncovered, for about 20 minutes or until mixture is thick. Cool mixture, then stir in egg.

TIPS Use coarsely grated kefalotyri cheese instead of provolone for an authentic Greek taste. Use a jar of store-bought béchamel or cheesy white sauce instead of the ricotta mixture if you like.

nutritional count per serving
▶ 45.8g total fat
▶ 23.2g saturated fat
▶ 3440kJ (823 cal)
▶ 51.6g carbohydrate
▶ 48.4g protein
▶ 4g fibre

3
WAYS
WITH MEAT
SAUCE

moussaka

PREP + COOK TIME 1¼ HOURS **SERVES** 6

1 quantity meat sauce (see tips)

16 slices char-grilled marinated eggplant

425g (13½-ounce) tub creamy béchamel pasta sauce

¼ cup (20g) finely grated provolone cheese

1 Preheat oven to 180°C/350°F. Oil a shallow 2.5-litre (10-cup) rectangular baking dish.

2 Place one-third of the eggplant, overlapping slices slightly, in baking dish; spread half the meat sauce over eggplant. Repeat layering with another third of the eggplant, remaining meat sauce then remaining eggplant. Spread béchamel sauce over top of eggplant; sprinkle with provolone.

3 Bake moussaka for about 40 minutes or until the top browns lightly. Cover; stand for 10 minutes before serving.

SERVING SUGGESTION Greek salad.

TIPS Make the meat sauce using the pastitsio recipe on pages 26-27, but omit the egg. Try to buy eggplant from a delicatessen or supermarket deli, as it is stored in less oil than bottled char-grilled eggplant; drain well on kitchen paper. You can replace the béchamel sauce with creamy carbonara pasta sauce; these are found in the refrigerated section of supermarkets.

nutritional count per serving
▶ 36.6g total fat
▶ 16.5g saturated fat
▶ 2420kJ (579 cal)
▶ 18g carbohydrate
▶ 41.8g protein
▶ 5.3g fibre

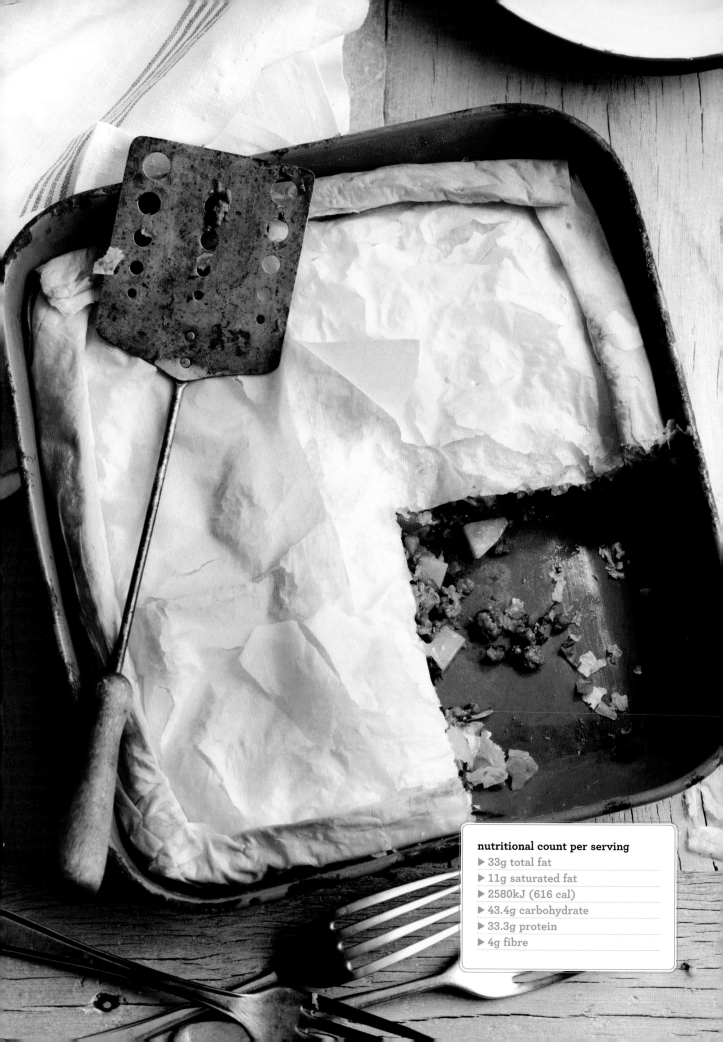

nutritional count per serving
- ▶ 33g total fat
- ▶ 11g saturated fat
- ▶ 2580kJ (616 cal)
- ▶ 43.4g carbohydrate
- ▶ 33.3g protein
- ▶ 4g fibre

3 WAYS WITH MEAT SAUCE

lamb fillo pie

PREP + COOK TIME 1 HOUR SERVES 4

1 quantity meat sauce (see tip)

½ x 750g (1½-pound) can tiny taters, chopped finely

1 cup (100g) coarsely grated provolone cheese

2 tablespoons finely chopped fresh mint

2 tablespoons finely chopped fresh oregano

15 sheets fillo pastry

¼ cup (60ml) olive oil

1 Stir potato, cheese and herbs into the meat sauce; season to taste.

2 Meanwhile, preheat oven to 220°C/425°F. Oil a medium shallow ovenproof dish.

3 Brush 1 sheet of pastry with a little oil; top with 4 more sheets, brushing each with more oil. Line dish with pastry. Repeat with another 5 sheets of pastry, and use to line opposite sides of the dish.

4 Spoon lamb mixture into dish. Layer remaining pastry sheets, brushing each with more oil; fold in half crossways. Cut pastry to fit top of dish; place on top of filling; fold overhanging pastry back over pie to enclose filling.

5 Bake pie for about 25 minutes or until browned.

SERVING SUGGESTIONS Green salad, and accompany with yoghurt, to drizzle.

TIP Make the meat sauce using the pastitsio recipe on pages 26-27, but omit the egg.

test kitchen tips

When working with the first five sheets of pastry, cover the remaining pastry with a sheet of baking paper then a damp clean tea towel to prevent it from drying out.

You can replace the provolone with greek kefalograviera cheese, if you can find it.

lamb schnitzel with caper herb mash and anchovy mayonnaise

PREP + COOK TIME 25 MINUTES SERVES 4

4 lamb steaks (600g)

¼ cup (35g) plain (all-purpose) flour

2 eggs, beaten lightly

1 tablespoon milk

2 cups (140g) stale breadcrumbs

½ cup (40g) finely grated parmesan

vegetable oil, for shallow-frying

600g (1¼-pound) tub mashed potato

2 tablespoons rinsed, drained baby capers, chopped finely

2 tablespoons finely chopped fresh chives

¼ cup coarsely chopped fresh flat-leaf parsley

½ cup (150g) aïoli

4 drained anchovy fillets, chopped finely

1 tablespoon warm water

1 Using a meat mallet, pound each steak between sheets of plastic wrap until 5mm (¼-inch) thick. Place flour in a medium shallow bowl; whisk egg and milk in another medium shallow bowl. Combine breadcrumbs and cheese in a third medium shallow bowl. Coat steaks, one at a time, in flour, then egg mixture, and finally breadcrumb mixture.

2 Heat oil in a large frying pan; shallow-fry schnitzels, in batches, until browned and cooked as desired. Remove from pan; drain on kitchen paper. Cover to keep warm.

3 Meanwhile, heat mash according to directions on packet. Stir in capers, chives and parsley.

4 Place aïoli, anchovy and the warm water in a small bowl; stir to combine. Divide caper herb mash and schnitzels among serving plates; drizzle with anchovy aïoli.

TIPS For a lemony anchovy aïoli, add 1 tablespoon of lemon juice to the anchovy mixture.

---

nutritional count per serving
- ▶ 69.8g total fat
- ▶ 26.6g saturated fat
- ▶ 4682kJ (1120 cal)
- ▶ 67.9g carbohydrate
- ▶ 52.7g protein
- ▶ 5.8g fibre

test kitchen tip

To get dinner on the table even faster,
use crumbed veal or chicken schnitzels.

za'atar crusted kebabs with hummus

PREP + COOK TIME 35 MINUTES SERVES 4

1 tablespoon olive oil

1 tablespoon lemon juice

800g (1½ pounds) diced lamb

¼ cup (35g) za'atar

8 pieces lavash (or other flat bread)

1⅓ cups (350g) hummus

½ cup coarsely chopped fresh flat-leaf parsley

¾ cup (200g) yoghurt

1 Combine oil and juice in a medium bowl, add lamb; toss lamb to coat in mixture. Thread lamb onto eight skewers.

2 Spread za'atar on an oven tray. Roll kebabs in za'atar until coated all over. Cook kebabs on a heated oiled grill plate until cooked as desired.

3 Serve kebabs on lavash; accompany with hummus, parsley and yoghurt.

TIPS Soak eight bamboo skewers in water before using to prevent them burning during cooking. Za'atar is a Middle-Eastern blend of roasted dried spices; it is available from Middle-Eastern food stores. It is easy to make at home: just combine 1 tablespoon sumac, 1 tablespoon toasted sesame seeds, 1 teaspoon dried marjoram and 2 teaspoons dried thyme in a small bowl.

nutritional count per serving

▶ 51.9g total fat
▶ 89.4g carbohydrate
▶ 15.7g saturated fat
▶ 65.2g protein
▶ 4661kJ (1113 cal)
▶ 12.4g fibre

mongolian lamb

PREP + COOK TIME 15 MINUTES **SERVES** 4

2 tablespoons peanut oil

600g (1¼ pounds) lamb stir-fry strips

1 medium brown onion (150g), cut into wedges

1 large red capsicum (bell pepper) (350g),
sliced thinly

120g (4-ounce) packet mongolian lamb
stir-fry sauce

200g (6½ ounces) snow peas, trimmed

3 green onions (scallions), sliced thinly

1 Heat half the oil in a wok; stir-fry lamb, in
batches, until browned. Remove from wok.
2 Heat remaining oil in wok; stir-fry brown onion
and capsicum until tender. Return lamb to wok with
sauce and peas; stir-fry until hot. Remove from
heat; stir in half the green onion, season to taste.
Serve sprinkled with remaining green onion.

SERVING SUGGESTION Steamed jasmine rice
or noodles.

TIPS To make your own stir-fry sauce mixture,
combine 2 tablespoons hoisin sauce, 1 tablespoon
oyster sauce and 2 tablespoons water in a small
jug. For a fuller flavour, marinate the lamb strips
for 3 hours or overnight in the fridge.

nutritional count per serving
- ▶ 16.5g total fat
- ▶ 3.7g saturated fat
- ▶ 1459kJ (349 cal)
- ▶ 15.4g carbohydrate
- ▶ 31.4g protein
- ▶ 4g fibre

lamb cutlets with char-grilled vegetable salad

PREP + COOK TIME 20 MINUTES SERVES 4

1-day-old bread roll (50g)

30g (1 ounce) each of pine nuts, macadamias and walnuts

½ cup (125ml) olive oil

olive-oil spray

12 french-trimmed lamb cutlets (600g)

⅓ cup (25g) finely grated parmesan

1 clove garlic, crushed

½ cup finely chopped fresh basil

2 tablespoons finely chopped fresh flat-leaf parsley

8 slices char-grilled zucchini

4 slices char-grilled eggplant, sliced thickly lengthways

2 char-grilled red capsicums (bell peppers), sliced thickly

1 Tear the bread roll into small pieces (about the same size as the nuts). Put the bread and nuts on an oven tray; drizzle with 1 tablespoon of the oil and rub well with your hands to coat all over.

2 Heat a large frying pan over medium-high heat; pan-fry the bread and nut mixture, stirring constantly, for about 5 minutes or until golden. Remove from pan immediately; spread out on an oven tray to cool.

3 Spray a large frying pan with the oil. Heat the pan over medium-high heat. Season the cutlets; cook for about 5 minutes or until cooked as you like them. Remove from pan; cover to keep warm.

4 Meanwhile, to make a chunky pesto, put the bread and nut mixture, remaining oil, parmesan, garlic and herbs in a large bowl; mix well. Season to taste. Serve lamb with vegetables and pesto.

TIP We used a mixture of walnuts, macadamias and pine nuts for this recipe but you can use any combination of nuts you like.

nutritional count per serving
▶ 60.7g total fat
▶ 10g saturated fat
▶ 2900kJ (693 cal)
▶ 12.9g carbohydrate
▶ 23.2g protein
▶ 5g fibre

SEAFOOD

seafood stew

PREP + COOK TIME 45 MINUTES SERVES 6

2 baby fennel bulbs (260g)

2 tablespoons lemon juice

1 tablespoon olive oil

2 medium brown onions (300g), chopped finely

4 cloves garlic, crushed

3 x 5cm (2¼-inch) strips thinly sliced orange rind

⅓ cup (80ml) dry white wine

1 teaspoon chilli flakes

pinch saffron threads

820g (26 ounces) canned diced tomatoes

1 litre (4 cups) fish stock

2kg (4 pounds) fresh seafood marinara mix

crusty bread and lemon zest, to serve

1 Trim fennel; reserve fronds. Using a V-slicer, mandoline, or a very sharp knife, slice the fennel as thinly as possible; combine with lemon juice in a small bowl.

2 Heat oil in a large saucepan; cook onion, stirring, until soft. Add garlic; cook, stirring, for 1 minute.

3 Stir rind, wine, chilli and saffron into onion mixture; cook, stirring, for 2 minutes. Add tomatoes; simmer, uncovered, for about 10 minutes or until mixture thickens slightly. Add stock; simmer, uncovered, for about 20 minutes or until liquid is reduced by about a quarter.

4 Add marinara mix to tomato mixture. Cover; simmer, stirring occasionally, for about 5 minutes or until prawns change colour and mussels open.

5 Serve stew topped with fennel mixture; sprinkle with reserved fronds and rind, accompany with bread.

TIP Some mussels might not open – these may need to be opened with a knife, or might not have cooked as quickly as the others. Farmed mussels will not all open up during cooking, and some will not open after excessive cooking – you do not have to discard these, just open with a knife and cook a little more, if you wish.

nutritional count per serving
▶ 17.2g total fat
▶ 3.5g saturated fat
▶ 2792kJ (668 cal)
▶ 63.7g carbohydrate
▶ 56.9g protein
▶ 9.2g fibre

fish and chips

PREP + COOK TIME 45 MINUTES (+ STANDING) **SERVES** 4

¼ cup (35g) plain (all-purpose) flour

¼ cup (35g) self-raising flour

⅓ cup (80ml) warm water

1 egg, separated

1kg (2 pounds) frozen thick-cut chips

vegetable oil, for deep frying

8 firm white fish fillets (960g)

⅔ cup (200g) tartare sauce

lemon cheeks or wedges, to serve

1 Sift flours into a medium bowl. Gradually whisk in the water and egg yolk until smooth. Cover; stand for 30 minutes.

2 Meanwhile, cook chips following packet directions.

3 Beat egg white in a small bowl with an electric mixer until soft peaks form. Fold egg white into batter, in two batches.

4 Fill a large saucepan or deep-fryer one-third full with oil; heat oil to 180°C/350°F (or until a small cube of white bread turns golden within 15 seconds). Dip fish in batter; drain excess. Deep-fry fish, in batches, until brown; drain. Serve fish with chips and tartare sauce; accompany with lemon cheeks.

SERVING SUGGESTION Green salad.

TIPS We used flathead fillets for this recipe. Tartare sauce can easily be made at home: Combine 2 tablespoons mayonnaise, 1 tablespoon buttermilk, 1 finely chopped shallot, 1 tablespoon finely chopped cornichons, 2 teaspoons finely chopped rinsed, drained capers, 2 teaspoons finely chopped fresh flat-leaf parsley and 2 teaspoons lemon juice in a small bowl.

nutritional count per serving
- ▶ 40g total fat
- ▶ 6.3g saturated fat
- ▶ 3465kJ (829 cal)
- ▶ 54.3g carbohydrate
- ▶ 60.1g protein
- ▶ 5.8g fibre

test kitchen tips

Kaffir lime leaves, aromatic leaves of a citrus tree, are used similarly to bay leaves or curry leaves. They are available from major supermarkets and Asian food stores. If you can't buy snake beans, use regular green beans. Laksa pastes vary in heat, so use only as much as suits your heat tolerance.

seafood laksa

PREP + COOK TIME 35 MINUTES SERVES 4

375g (12 ounces) dried rice noodles

3¼ cups (810ml) coconut milk

½ cup (120g) laksa paste

4 fresh kaffir lime leaves, torn

2 tablespoons peanut oil

750g (1½ pounds) fresh seafood marinara mix

500g (1 pound) uncooked shelled medium king prawns (shrimp)

200g (6½ ounces) snake beans, chopped coarsely

½ cup loosely packed fresh thai basil leaves

½ cup (70g) coarsely chopped roasted unsalted peanuts

2 fresh long red chillies, sliced thinly

1 Place noodles in a large heatproof bowl, cover with boiling water; stand until tender, drain.

2 Meanwhile, place coconut milk, paste and lime leaves in a wok; simmer, stirring, for about 15 minutes or until mixture reduces by a third.

3 Meanwhile, heat oil in a large frying pan; cook marinara mix and prawns, in batches, until just changed in colour. Drain on kitchen paper.

4 Add beans and seafood to curry mixture in wok; cook, uncovered, stirring occasionally, for about 5 minutes or until beans are just tender and seafood is cooked as desired.

5 Divide noodles into serving bowls; top with curry, sprinkle with basil, nuts and chilli.

nutritional count per serving
- 64.3g total fat
- 39.8g saturated fat
- 3716kJ (889 cal)
- 18.3g carbohydrate
- 57.1g protein
- 7.2g fibre

smoked trout and crisp noodle salad

PREP TIME 20 MINUTES **SERVES** 4

450g (14 ounces) smoked ocean trout fillets

500g (1-pound) packet shredded coleslaw mix

2 x 100g (3-ounce) packets crispy fried noodles

4 green onions (scallions), sliced thinly

2 tablespoons toasted sesame seeds

½ cup (125ml) sweet chilli sauce

1 tablespoon sesame oil

2 tablespoons white wine vinegar

2 tablespoons japanese soy sauce

1 Discard the skin and bones from the fish. Flake fish into a large bowl; add coleslaw mix, noodles, onion and sesame seeds.

2 Place remaining ingredients in a screw-top jar; shake well. Drizzle dressing over salad; toss gently.

TIPS Filleted portions of smoked trout, in a variety of sizes, are now available at most supermarkets; we used three 150g (4½-ounce) portions for this recipe.
Crispy fried noodles are crisp wheat noodles already deep-fried. They are available from Asian grocery stores and most major supermarkets.
If you like, replace the coleslaw mix with 3½ cups of finely shredded red or white cabbage and 2 coarsely grated medium carrots.

nutritional count per serving
- ► 20.8g total fat
- ► 5.4g saturated fat
- ► 1814kJ (434 cal)
- ► 23.1g carbohydrate
- ► 34.8g protein
- ► 7.1g fibre

prawn and chive dumpling soup

PREP + COOK TIME 25 MINUTES **SERVES** 4

1 litre (4 cups) water

1 litre (4 cups) fish stock

10cm (4-inch) stick fresh lemon grass (20g), halved lengthways

2 fresh kaffir lime leaves

20 frozen prawn and chive dumplings

1 tablespoon light soy sauce

1 tablespoon lime juice

500g (1 pound) baby buk choy, chopped coarsely

1 cup (80g) bean sprouts

¼ cup loosely packed fresh coriander leaves (cilantro)

1 fresh small red thai (serrano) chilli, sliced finely

1 Combine the water, stock, lemon grass and lime leaves in a large saucepan; bring to the boil. Reduce heat; simmer broth, uncovered, for 15 minutes. Discard lemon grass and lime leaves.

2 Return broth to the boil; add dumplings. Simmer, uncovered, for about 5 minutes or until dumplings are cooked through. Stir in sauce and juice.

3 Divide buk choy between serving bowls; ladle over hot broth and dumplings. Serve topped with sprouts, coriander and chilli.

TIP Baby buk choy is also known as pak kat farang or shanghai bok choy, and is much smaller, and more tender, than buk choy. Its mildly acrid but appealing taste, has made it one of the most commonly used Asian greens. It can be found at most greengrocers, especially Asian greengrocers, and many larger supermarkets.

nutritional count per serving

▶ 5.4g total fat   ▶ 31g carbohydrate

▶ 2.1g saturated fat ▶ 18g protein

▶ 1062kJ (254 cal)   ▶ 3.7g fibre

smoked salmon and mascarpone crêpe cake

PREP + COOK TIME 30 MINUTES (+ REFRIGERATION) SERVES 8

2 cups (500g) mascarpone

2 tablespoons prepared horseradish

2 tablespoons rinsed, drained capers, chopped coarsely

2 tablespoons finely chopped fresh tarragon

1 tablespoon finely grated lemon rind

8 frozen french-style crêpes (400g), thawed

600g (1¼ pounds) sliced smoked salmon

MIXED PEA SALAD

300g (9½ ounces) sugar snap peas, trimmed

200g (6½ ounces) snow peas, trimmed

150g (4½ ounces) snow pea tendrils

2 tablespoons olive oil

2 tablespoons lemon juice

1 Line base and side of a deep 22cm (8¾-inch) round cake pan with plastic wrap. Combine mascarpone, horseradish, capers, tarragon and rind in a medium bowl; stir well.

2 Place one crêpe in the cake pan; spread with about ⅓ cup of the mascarpone mixture, cover with slices of salmon. Continue layering with remaining crêpes, mascarpone mixture and salmon, finishing with a crêpe layer. Cover; refrigerate 3 hours or until firm.

3 Make mixed pea salad.

4 Cut crêpe cake into eight wedges; serve with mixed pea salad.

MIXED PEA SALAD Boil, steam or microwave sugar snap and snow peas, separately, until just tender; drain. Rinse under cold water; drain. Place in a large bowl with remaining ingredients; toss gently to combine.

TIPS If the mascarpone is too soft, the refrigeration time may need to be increased to firm up the crêpe cake. This recipe can be assembled the day before; store, covered, in the fridge.

nutritional count per serving
▶ 39.7g total fat
▶ 21.9g saturated fat
▶ 2298kJ (549 cal)
▶ 23.6g carbohydrate
▶ 24.4g protein
▶ 1.9g fibre

garlic prawn and basil pizzas

PREP + COOK TIME 20 MINUTES **MAKES** 4

4 pocket pitta breads (270g)

⅔ cup (180g) tomato and basil pasta sauce

500g (1 pound) uncooked shelled medium garlic king prawns (shrimp)

¼ teaspoon dried chilli flakes

⅔ cup coarsely torn fresh basil leaves

1 Preheat oven to 220°C/425°F. Place two oven trays in oven to heat up.

2 Place two pitta breads on each tray; spread evenly with sauce. Top with prawns and sprinkle with chilli. Bake for about 12 minutes or until bases are crisp and prawns are cooked; sprinkle with basil.

test kitchen tips

Garlic prawns can be purchased pre-marinated from most fishmongers, but they can be easily marinated at home: Combine 4 crushed garlic cloves and 1 tablespoon olive oil with 500g shelled uncooked medium king prawns in a large bowl. To jazz up the pizzas, add a little crumbled fetta or sliced cherry tomatoes to the pizzas before baking. These are great topped with baby rocket (arugula) tossed in olive oil and lemon juice.

nutritional count per pizza
- ▶ 3.4g total fat
- ▶ 0.5g saturated fat
- ▶ 619kJ (148 cal)
- ▶ 17.6g carbohydrate
- ▶ 10.7g protein
- ▶ 1.6g fibre

one pot chilli, tomato and garlic prawn spaghetti

PREP + COOK TIME 25 MINUTES SERVES 4

This dish is so simple, requiring very little preparation, and the pasta and the sauce are cooked together in the one pot, meaning less washing up.

1 tablespoon olive oil

1 medium brown onion (150g), chopped finely

2 cloves garlic, crushed

1 fresh long red chilli, chopped finely

400g (12½ ounces) canned diced tomatoes

⅓ cup coarsely chopped fresh basil

1 litre (4 cups) water

500g (1 pound) spaghetti

500g (1 pound) uncooked shelled medium prawns (shrimp)

2 tablespoons olive oil, extra

⅓ cup small fresh basil leaves

1 Heat oil in a large saucepan; cook onion, garlic and chilli, stirring, until onion softens. Add tomatoes and chopped basil; cook, stirring, 1 minute.

2 Add the water to the pan; bring to the boil. Add pasta; once pasta begins to soften, gently mix into the tomato mixture. Boil, uncovered, stirring, for 5 minutes. Add prawns; boil, uncovered, stirring, for about 5 minutes or until pasta is tender and prawns just change colour. Season to taste.

3 Serve bowls of pasta drizzled with extra oil and sprinkled with basil leaves.

TIPS This recipe is quite versatile – here we used prawns but you could easily change this basic sauce recipe to suit your tastes and needs. You could use the same amount of marinara mix or shredded barbecued chicken instead of the prawns. For a vegetarian option, instead of the prawns try adding some char-grilled eggplant or marinated antipasto vegetables and fresh rocket at the end of step 2. Another variation is to cook some thinly sliced bacon with the onion mixture in step 1 to make spaghetti amatriciana.

nutritional count per serving
- ▶ 15.9g total fat
- ▶ 2.4g saturated fat
- ▶ 2873kJ (686 cal)
- ▶ 89.9g carbohydrate
- ▶ 41.1g protein
- ▶ 6.6g fibre

BEEF

veal parmigiana

PREP + COOK TIME 1¾ HOURS SERVES 4

30g (1 ounce) butter

⅓ cup (80ml) olive oil

4 crumbed veal schnitzels (600g)

1½ cups (150g) coarsely grated mozzarella

⅓ cup (25g) finely grated parmesan

TOMATO SAUCE

1 tablespoon olive oil

1 medium brown onion (150g), chopped finely

1 stalk celery (150g), trimmed, chopped finely

1 medium red capsicum (bell pepper) (200g), chopped finely

1 clove garlic, crushed

2 cups (520g) bottled tomato pasta sauce (passata)

2 teaspoons white (granulated) sugar

½ cup (125ml) chicken stock

1 tablespoon finely chopped fresh basil

1 Make tomato sauce.

2 Preheat oven to 180°C/350°F.

3 Heat butter and half the oil in a large flameproof dish; cook veal, in batches, on stove top, until browned both sides.

4 Return veal to dish; top with mozzarella, drizzle with tomato sauce then sprinkle with parmesan. Drizzle over remaining oil.

5 Transfer to oven; bake, uncovered, for about 20 minutes or until browned lightly. Serve with steamed green beans, or a green salad, if you like.

TOMATO SAUCE Heat oil in a medium frying pan; cook onion, celery, capsicum and garlic, stirring, until onion softens. Add pasta sauce, sugar and stock. Cover; bring to the boil. Reduce heat; simmer, uncovered, for about 5 minutes or until sauce is thick. Stir in basil. Season to taste.

3 WAYS WITH BOLOGNESE

Make this big batch of bolognese sauce one night, and dinner is taken care of for two more nights – 1 recipe = 3 dinners.

fettuccine bolognese

PREP + COOK TIME 1½ HOURS **SERVES** 4

2 tablespoons olive oil

2 large brown onions (400g), chopped finely

4 cloves garlic, crushed

1.5kg (3 pounds) minced (ground) beef

½ cup (140g) tomato paste

2½ cups (625ml) beef stock

2kg (4 pounds) canned diced tomatoes

¼ cup finely chopped fresh oregano

375g (12 ounces) fettuccine

½ cup (40g) flaked parmesan cheese

1 Heat oil in a large saucepan; cook onion and garlic, stirring, until onion softens.
2 Add beef to pan; cook, stirring, until browned. Add paste, stock and tomatoes; bring to the boil. Reduce heat; simmer, covered, for 30 minutes. Uncover; simmer for a further 45 minutes or until sauce is thickened. Remove from heat; stir in oregano. Season to taste.
3 Meanwhile, cook pasta in a large saucepan of boiling water until tender; drain.
4 Serve 6 cups of the bolognese mixture with the pasta, sprinkle bowls of pasta with parmesan.
5 Reserve remaining bolognese for later use (see tips).

TIPS You need 6 cups of bolognese mixture for the tomato, beef and pea lasagne recipe (page 56) and 2 cups of bolognese mixture for the stuffed eggplants recipe (page 59). Store the sauce, covered, in the refrigerator for up to 3 days or freeze portions in airtight containers for up to 3 months.
You can use 2 teaspoons dried oregano instead of the fresh if you prefer or if fresh is unavailable. We used fettuccine in this recipe, but you can use the pasta of your choice.

nutritional count per serving
▶ 30.9g total fat
▶ 12.6g saturated fat
▶ 3491kJ (834 cal)
▶ 76g carbohydrate
▶ 58.2g protein
▶ 7.5g fibre

tomato, beef and pea lasagne

PREP + COOK TIME 1¼ HOURS **SERVES** 8

6 cups bolognese sauce (page 55)

1 cup (120g) frozen peas

500g (1 pound) soft ricotta

1½ cups (375ml) milk

1 egg

1½ cups (150g) pizza cheese

4 fresh lasagne sheets

1 Preheat oven to 200°C/400°F. Oil deep 3-litre (12-cup) ovenproof dish.
2 Reheat bolognese mixture in a large saucepan over medium-high heat until hot. Stir in peas.
3 Whisk ricotta, milk and egg in a medium bowl until smooth. Stir in half the pizza cheese.

4 Line the base of the dish with lasagne sheets, trimming to fit. Top with half the bolognese sauce, one-third of the cheese sauce, then more lasagne sheets, trimming to fit. Top with remaining bolognese sauce, half the remaining cheese sauce and lasagne sheets, trimming to fit. Top with remaining cheese sauce; sprinkle with remaining pizza cheese.
5 Cover lasagne with foil; bake for 35 minutes. Uncover; bake a further 20 minutes or until browned lightly. Stand for 10 minutes before serving.

TIP You could use a 425g (13½-ounce) tub of creamy béchamel pasta sauce instead of the ricotta mixture.

nutritional count per serving
▶ 24.8g total fat
▶ 12.4g saturated fat
▶ 1866kJ (446 cal)
▶ 17.2g carbohydrate
▶ 37g protein
▶ 3.6g fibre

test kitchen tip

This recipe uses four lasagne
sheets but only has three
pasta layers. We used the
fourth sheet to trim and fill
any gaps in each pasta layer.

test kitchen tip

You can use ricotta cheese
instead of the fetta for a more
authentic Italian taste.

stuffed eggplants

PREP + COOK TIME 45 MINUTES SERVES 4

2 medium eggplants (600g)

1 tablespoon olive oil

2 cups bolognese sauce (page 55)

1 teaspoon finely grated lemon rind

1 tablespoon lemon juice

2 tablespoons finely chopped fresh flat-leaf parsley

100g (3 ounces) soft fetta, crumbled

⅓ cup (25g) stale breadcrumbs

1 Preheat oven to 200°C/400°F. Oil medium shallow baking dish.

2 Meanwhile, cook eggplants in a large saucepan of boiling water for 6 minutes; drain. When cool enough to handle, halve lengthways.

3 Using a small sharp knife, carefully remove flesh from eggplant halves, leaving a 1cm (½ inch) border; chop flesh finely.

4 Heat oil in a large frying pan; cook eggplant flesh, stirring, until flesh is tender. Add bolognese sauce; cook, stirring, until hot. Remove from heat; stir in rind, juice and half the parsley. Season to taste.

5 Place eggplant halves in dish; fill with beef mixture. Sprinkle with combined remaining parsley, fetta and breadcrumbs. Bake, uncovered, for about 30 minutes or until eggplants are tender.

SERVING SUGGESTION Green salad.

nutritional count per serving
▶ 19.8g total fat
▶ 7.9g saturated fat
▶ 1346kJ (322 cal)
▶ 11.5g carbohydrate
▶ 21.6g protein
▶ 5.8g fibre

3 WAYS WITH SLOPPY JOES

sloppy joes

PREP + COOK TIME 1½ HOURS SERVES 4

4 medium potatoes (800g), unpeeled

2 tablespoons olive oil

2 large brown onions (400g), chopped finely

3 cloves garlic, crushed

2 medium carrots (240g), chopped finely

2 medium red capsicums (bell peppers) (400g), chopped finely

3 stalks celery (450g), trimmed, chopped finely

1.5kg (3 pounds) minced (ground) beef

¼ cup (70g) mild american-style mustard

1½ cups (375ml) tomato sauce (ketchup)

1 cup (250ml) beef stock

1 tablespoon finely chopped fresh flat-leaf parsley

1 Preheat oven to 220°C/425°F.

2 Wrap potatoes in foil; place in a small shallow baking dish. Bake about 1 hour or until tender.

3 Meanwhile, heat oil in a large saucepan; cook onion, garlic, carrot, capsicum and celery, stirring, until vegetables soften. Add beef; stir until browned.

4 Add mustard, sauce and stock to pan; stir for about 10 minutes or until sauce thickens. Season to taste.

5 Unwrap potatoes; cut into thick slices, without cutting all the way through.

6 To serve, divide a third (about 4 cups) of the beef mixture evenly over potatoes; sprinkle with parsley. Reserve the remaining meat mixture for later use (see tips).

Make this batch of sloppy joe mixture one night, and dinner is taken care of for two more nights – 1 recipe = 3 dinners.

TIPS You need about 4 cups of the sloppy joe mixture for the meat pies recipe (page 63) and about 4 cups of sloppy joe mixture for the cottage pie recipe (page 63). Store the sloppy joe mixture, covered, in the refrigerator for up to 3 days or freeze portions in airtight containers for up to 3 months.
To save time, and to avoid chopping all the vegies, use the same weight of frozen mixed diced vegetables.

nutritional count per serving
▶ 20.5g total fat
▶ 8g saturated fat
▶ 2095kJ (501 cal)
▶ 37g carbohydrate
▶ 38.3g protein
▶ 6.7g fibre

3 WAYS WITH SLOPPY JOES

meat pies

PREP + COOK TIME 45 MINUTES **MAKES** 4

4 cups sloppy joe mixture (page 60)

5 sheets ready-rolled shortcrust pastry

1 egg, beaten lightly

1 Preheat oven to 200°C/400°F. Oil four ¾-cup (180ml) pie dishes.
2 Cut four 15cm (6-inch) rounds and four 12cm (5-inch) rounds from pastry; press large rounds into base and sides of pie dishes.
3 Divide sloppy joe mixture between pie cases, brush edges with a little egg; top with small pastry rounds, pressing edges together firmly to seal. Brush pies with egg, make small cuts in pastry tops.
4 Bake pies about 30 minutes or until browned lightly and heated through.

cottage pie

PREP + COOK TIME 35 MINUTES **SERVES** 4

4 cups sloppy joe mixture (page 60)

600g (1¼ pounds) potatoes, chopped coarsely

30g (1 ounce) butter

⅓ cup (80ml) hot milk

1 cup (120g) frozen peas

1 tablespoon worcestershire sauce

¼ cup finely chopped fresh flat-leaf parsley

¾ cup (100g) coarsely grated cheddar

1 Boil, steam or microwave potato until tender; drain. Mash potato in a large bowl with butter and milk until smooth, season to taste.
2 Meanwhile, reheat sloppy joe mixture in a large saucepan over medium-high heat until hot; stir in peas, sauce and parsley.
3 Preheat grill (broiler).
4 Spoon sloppy joe mixture into an oiled 2-litre (8-cup) ovenproof dish; spread potato mixture over top. Sprinkle cheese over potato. Grill pie for about 5 minutes or until browned lightly.

SERVING SUGGESTION Baby green peas.

(photograph page 64)

---

nutritional count per pie
▶ 31.8g total fat
▶ 13.7g saturated fat
▶ 2327kJ (556 cal)
▶ 28.8g carbohydrate
▶ 37.7g protein
▶ 3.9g fibre

---

nutritional count per serving
▶ 35.2g total fat
▶ 17.7g saturated fat
▶ 2728kJ (652 cal)
▶ 34.4g carbohydrate
▶ 45.6g protein
▶ 7.9g fibre

cottage pie (see recipe page 63)

steak sandwich with beetroot salsa (see recipe page 66)

steak sandwich with beetroot salsa

PREP + COOK TIME 25 MINUTES MAKES 4

2 teaspoons olive oil

4 thin beef scotch fillet steaks (500g)

30g (1 ounce) baby rocket leaves (arugula)

2 medium tomatoes (300g), sliced thickly

½ cup (140g) caramelised onions

½ cup (150g) aïoli

4 small turkish bread rolls (660g), halved, toasted

BEETROOT SALSA

1 large beetroot (beet) (200g), peeled, grated coarsely

2 teaspoons wholegrain (seeded) mustard

2 teaspoons lemon juice

2 teaspoons olive oil

1 Make beetroot salsa.
2 Meanwhile, heat oil in a large frying pan; cook steaks 2-3 minutes each side or until cooked as you like. Cover; stand for 5 minutes.
3 Sandwich caramelised onion, steaks, beetroot salsa, tomato, rocket and aïoli between toast slices.

BEETROOT SALSA Combine ingredients in a medium bowl; season.

TIPS Aïoli can be made easily at home: Combine ½ cup whole-egg mayonnaise and 1 crushed garlic clove in a small bowl. Season to taste.

(photograph page 65)

nutritional count per sandwich
- ▶ 31.8g total fat
- ▶ 6.3g saturated fat
- ▶ 3732kJ (891 cal)
- ▶ 94.3g carbohydrate
- ▶ 44.4g protein
- ▶ 2.7g fibre

hokkien mee with beef

PREP + COOK TIME 20 MINUTES SERVES 4

300g (9½ ounces) hokkien noodles

1 tablespoon peanut oil

700g (1½ pounds) beef strips

1 medium brown onion (150g), sliced thinly

2.5cm (1-inch) piece fresh ginger (15g), grated

2 cloves garlic, crushed

2 fresh small red thai (serrano) chillies, sliced thinly

400g (12½ ounces) packaged fresh stir-fry vegetables

2 tablespoons hoisin sauce

1 tablespoon dark soy sauce

1 Place noodles in a medium heatproof bowl, cover with boiling water; separate with a fork, drain.
2 Heat half the oil in a wok; stir-fry beef, in batches, until browned. Remove from wok.
3 Heat remaining oil in wok; stir-fry onion until soft. Add ginger, garlic and chilli; stir-fry until fragrant. Add vegetables; stir-fry until tender.
4 Return beef to wok with noodles and sauces; stir-fry until heated through.

TIP Dark soy sauce is deep brown, almost black in colour; it is rich, with a thicker consistency than other types. Pungent but not particularly salty, it is good for marinating. Available from Asian supermarkets.

nutritional count per serving
- ▶ 17.4g total fat
- ▶ 6.2g saturated fat
- ▶ 1927kJ (461 cal)
- ▶ 27.2g carbohydrate
- ▶ 46.1g protein
- ▶ 5.3g fibre

hokkien mee with beef

3 WAYS WITH CHILLI CON CARNE

chilli con carne

PREP + COOK TIME 1¼ HOURS SERVES 4

2 tablespoons olive oil

2 large brown onions (400g), chopped finely

3 cloves garlic, crushed

1.5kg (3 pounds) minced (ground) beef

2 x 60g (2-ounce) sachets taco seasoning

3 cups (750ml) beef stock

½ cup (140g) tomato paste

3 x 800g (1½-pound) cans crushed tomatoes

¼ cup finely chopped fresh oregano

3 x 400g (12½-ounce) cans kidney beans, rinsed, drained

200g (6½ ounces) guacamole (see tips)

4 flour tortillas (240g), warmed

1 Heat oil in a large saucepan; cook onion and garlic, stirring, until onion softens. Add beef and taco seasoning; stir until browned. Stir in stock, paste, tomatoes and oregano; bring to the boil. Reduce heat; simmer, covered, for 30 minutes.

2 Stir beans into beef mixture; simmer, uncovered, for a further 45 minutes or until thickened slightly. Season to taste.

3 Serve one-third (about 5 cups) of chilli con carne mixture with guacamole and tortillas. Accompany with sour cream, if you like.

4 Reserve remaining chilli con carne for later use (see tips).

Make this big batch of chilli con carne one night, and dinner is taken care of for two more nights – 1 recipe = 3 dinners.

TIPS You need about 5 cups of chilli con carne mixture for the beef enchiladas recipe (page 70) and about 5 cups of chilli con carne mixture for the beef and bean nachos recipe (page 73). Store the chilli con carne mixture, covered, in the refrigerator for up to 3 days or freeze portions in airtight containers for up to 3 months.
You can use 2 teaspoons dried oregano instead of the fresh if you prefer or if fresh is unavailable.
For a bit of a twist, we've served our chilli con carne with an avocado salad: Combine 1 coarsely chopped large avocado, 125g (4 ounces) halved yellow grape tomatoes, 1 thinly sliced small red onion, 1 finely chopped fresh long red chilli and ¼ cup loosely packed coriander leaves (cilantro) in a large bowl; toss gently.

nutritional count per serving
▶ 29.2g total fat
▶ 10.6g saturated fat
▶ 2445kJ (584 cal)
▶ 33g carbohydrate
▶ 42.1g protein
▶ 10.5g fibre

3 WAYS WITH CHILLI CON CARNE

beef enchiladas

PREP + COOK TIME 45 MINUTES **MAKES** 10

5 cups chilli con carne mixture (page 68)

1½ cups (240g) coarsely grated cheddar

10 x 15cm (6-inch) flour tortillas

750g (1½ pounds) medium chunky tomato salsa

⅔ cup (160g) sour cream

1 Preheat oven to 180°C/350°F. Oil a shallow rectangular 3-litre (12-cup) ovenproof dish.
2 Combine chilli con carne mixture and a third of the cheese in a medium bowl.
3 Heat tortillas according to directions on packet; place on a board. Place ½ cup of the chilli con carne mixture along the edge of each tortilla; roll firmly to enclose filling.
4 Spread ½ cup tomato salsa into dish. Place enchiladas, seam-side down, in dish (they should fit snugly, without overcrowding). Pour over the remaining tomato salsa; sprinkle enchiladas with remaining cheese.
5 Bake enchiladas, uncovered, for about 15 minutes or until cheese melts and enchiladas are heated through. Serve with sour cream; sprinkle with coriander leaves (cilantro), if you like.

nutritional count per enchilada
▶ 24.5g total fat
▶ 13.3g saturated fat
▶ 1788kJ (427 cal)
▶ 24.2g carbohydrate
▶ 25g protein
▶ 5.5g fibre

test kitchen tip

We used a medium tomato salsa but you can use a mild or hot salsa, depending on your chilli tolerance.

3 WAYS WITH CHILLI CON CARNE

beef and bean nachos

PREP + COOK TIME 45 MINUTES **SERVES** 4

5 cups chilli con carne mixture (page 68)

1 medium avocado (250g), chopped coarsely

1 tablespoon lime juice

200g (6½ ounces) corn chips (tortilla chips)

1 cup (120g) coarsely grated cheddar

½ cup (120g) sour cream

1 medium tomato (150g), chopped finely

2 tablespoons fresh coriander leaves (cilantro), sliced finely

1 Reheat chilli con carne mixture in a large saucepan over medium-high heat until hot.
2 Meanwhile, mash avocado in a small bowl with juice until smooth; season to taste.
3 Preheat grill (broiler).
4 Divide corn chips between four heatproof serving bowls; sprinkle with cheese. Grill, in batches, until cheese melts, then evenly top with chilli con carne mixture, avocado mixture, sour cream, tomato and coriander.

nutritional count per serving
▶ 59.8g total fat
▶ 27.1g saturated fat
▶ 3699kJ (885 cal)
▶ 40.2g carbohydrate
▶ 42g protein
▶ 11.8g fibre

PORK

nasi goreng

PREP + COOK TIME 40 MINUTES SERVES 4

2 tablespoons peanut oil

250g (8 ounces) pork fillet, sliced thinly

1 medium brown onion (150g), sliced thinly

1 medium red capsicum (bell pepper) (200g),
sliced thinly

3 fresh long red chillies, sliced thinly

2 cloves garlic, crushed

2.5cm (1-inch) piece fresh ginger (10g), grated

1 teaspoon shrimp paste

450g (14½-ounce) packaged microwave white
long-grain rice

250g (8 ounces) cooked shelled small king prawns
(shrimp)

1 tablespoon kecap manis

6 green onions (scallions), sliced thinly

4 eggs

¼ cup (35g) roasted unsalted peanuts,
chopped coarsely

lime wedges, to serve

1 Heat half the oil in a wok; stir-fry pork, in batches,
until browned. Remove from wok.
2 Heat remaining oil in wok; stir-fry brown onion,
capsicum, chilli, garlic, ginger and paste until
vegetables soften. Add rice; stir-fry until combined.
3 Return pork to wok with prawns, kecap manis
and half the green onion; stir-fry until hot. Divide
evenly among serving bowls; cover to keep warm.
4 Meanwhile, fry eggs in wok until whites set. Top
each bowl of rice with an egg then sprinkle with
nuts and remaining green onion. Accompany with
lime wedges.

TIPS To save time use sliced barbecued pork
(available from Asian food stores) instead of
the pork fillet. This recipe is a great way to use
up leftover rice.

Traditionally eaten throughout Malaysia and Indonesia at breakfast to use up the cold rice from the day before, this famous fried rice dish can be made with beef, chicken, tofu or vegetables as well as the pork and prawns used here.

quiche lorraine

PREP + COOK TIME 1 HOUR (+ REFRIGERATION) SERVES 6

2 sheets shortcrust pastry

1 medium brown onion (150g), chopped finely

200g (6½ ounces) diced bacon

3 eggs

300ml pouring cream

½ cup (125ml) milk

¾ cup (120g) coarsely grated gruyère

1 Overlap pastry sheets slightly; roll between sheets of baking paper until the overlap is flattened and both sheets are firmly joined. Line the base and side of a deep 24cm (9½-inch) round loose-based flan pan with pastry sheet, trimming to fit; refrigerate for 30 minutes.

2 Preheat oven to 200°C/400°F.

3 Place pan on an oven tray, line pastry with baking paper; fill with dried beans or rice. Bake for 10 minutes; carefully remove paper and rice. Bake for a further 5 minutes or until pastry case is browned. Cool slightly.

4 Reduce oven temperature to 180°C/350°F.

5 Meanwhile, heat a small oiled frying pan over medium-high heat; cook onion and bacon, stirring, until onion softens; drain on kitchen paper. Sprinkle bacon mixture over pastry case.

6 Whisk eggs in a large jug then whisk in cream, milk and gruyère, season; pour into pastry case.

7 Bake quiche about 35 minutes or until set. Stand in pan for 5 minutes before serving.

TIP With origins as far back as 16th century France, quiche is now enjoyed worldwide. The name comes from the German word 'kuchen' meaning cake. While now made using shortcrust or puff pastry, quiche was originally made using bread dough.

nutritional count per serving
▶ 51.8g total fat
▶ 35.4g saturated fat
▶ 3139kJ (751 cal)
▶ 35.4g carbohydrate
▶ 22.1g protein
▶ 2g fibre

gingered pork with vegetables

PREP + COOK TIME 25 MINUTES (+ REFRIGERATION) SERVES 4

700g (1½ pounds) pork strips

10cm (4-inch) piece fresh ginger (50g), grated

¼ cup coarsely chopped fresh coriander (cilantro)

2 tablespoons rice vinegar

2 tablespoons peanut oil

400g (12½ ounces) packaged fresh stir-fry vegetables

2 tablespoons light soy sauce

150g (4½ ounces) baby spinach leaves

3 cups (240g) bean sprouts

½ cup loosely packed fresh coriander leaves (cilantro), extra

1 Combine pork in a medium bowl with ginger, chopped coriander and vinegar. Cover; refrigerate 1 hour.

2 Heat half the oil in a wok; stir-fry pork mixture, in batches, until pork is cooked through. Remove from wok.

3 Heat remaining oil in wok; stir-fry vegetables until just tender; remove from wok. Return pork to wok with sauce; stir-fry until hot. Return cooked vegetables to wok with spinach, sprouts and extra coriander; stir-fry until spinach just wilts.

TIP For a more intense flavour, marinate the pork for 3 hours or overnight.

nutritional count per serving
- ▶ 12.6g total fat
- ▶ 2.6g saturated fat
- ▶ 1463kJ (350 cal)
- ▶ 10.3g carbohydrate
- ▶ 45.9g protein
- ▶ 5.7g fibre

teriyaki pork with pineapple

PREP + COOK TIME 40 MINUTES (+ REFRIGERATION) **SERVES** 4

½ cup (125ml) teriyaki marinade

600g (1¼ pounds) pork fillets

1 small pineapple (900g), sliced thinly

2 green onions (scallions), sliced thinly

1 Combine marinade and pork in a medium bowl, turn to coat in marinade. Cover; refrigerate 1 hour.

2 Drain pork; reserve marinade. Cook pork on a heated oiled grill plate (or grill or barbecue) until browned and cooked as desired. Cover; stand for 10 minutes, then slice thinly.

3 Cook pineapple on same grill plate for 2 minutes or until soft.

4 Bring reserved marinade to the boil in a small saucepan; boil for 5 minutes or until marinade reduces by half.

5 Serve pork with pineapple and onion; drizzle with marinade.

TIPS For a fuller flavour, marinate the pork for 3 hours or overnight. Teriyaki sauce is available from the supermarket, but it's very easy to make to home: Combine ¼ cup japanese soy sauce, 2 tablespoons cooking sake, ⅓ cup mirin and 2 teaspoons white sugar.
Because it contains raw meat juices, the marinade must be boiled for the time stated.

nutritional count per serving
▸ 12.2g total fat ▸ 13.3g carbohydrate
▸ 4.1g saturated fat ▸ 34.1g protein
▸ 1371kJ (328 cal) ▸ 3g fibre

warm beetroot and lentil salad with pork sausages

PREP + COOK TIME 45 MINUTES SERVES 4

850g (1¾ pounds) small beetroots (beets)

2 x 400g (12-ounce) cans brown lentils, rinsed, drained

1 tablespoon olive oil

1 large brown onion (200g), chopped finely

2 teaspoons yellow mustard seeds

2 teaspoons ground cumin

1 teaspoon ground coriander

½ cup (125ml) chicken stock

150g (4½ ounces) baby spinach leaves

½ cup (125ml) french dressing

8 thick pork sausages (960g)

1 Discard leaves and all but 2.5cm (1-inch) of the stalk from each beetroot. Boil, steam or microwave unpeeled beetroots for about 20 minutes or until just tender; drain. When cool enough to handle, peel then quarter beetroots; place in a large bowl with lentils.

2 Heat oil in a large frying pan; cook onion, seeds and spices, stirring, until onion softens. Add stock; bring to the boil. Remove from heat; stir in spinach.

3 Add spinach mixture and dressing to beetroot and lentil mixture in bowl; mix gently to combine. Season to taste.

4 Cook sausages in same cleaned pan. When cool enough to handle, slice sausages; serve with salad.

TIPS Using canned lentils instead of dried really reduces the cooking time in this recipe.
If you like, you can make your own simple dressing for this salad: Combine 1 teaspoon fresh thyme leaves, 1 crushed garlic clove, ¼ cup olive oil and ½ cup red wine vinegar in a screw-top jar; shake well.

test kitchen tip

Speed up this recipe further
by using a 450g (14½-ounce)
can of baby beetroot, drained
and quartered, instead of
cooking the fresh beetroot.

nutritional count per serving
▶ 86g total fat
▶ 31g saturated fat
▶ 4992kJ (1193 cal)
▶ 44.8g carbohydrate
▶ 53.8g protein
▶ 16.6g fibre

nutritional count per serving
- ▶ 39.9g total fat
- ▶ 15.2g saturated fat
- ▶ 3210kJ (768 cal)
- ▶ 44.4g carbohydrate
- ▶ 53.6g protein
- ▶ 8g fibre

test kitchen tip

There are many good barbecue marinades available in supermarkets today; you could use a smoky barbecue sauce marinade instead of the barbecue sauce in this recipe, just add a little vegetable oil, to prevent it sticking to the barbecue or grill plate.

barbecued pork spare ribs with red cabbage coleslaw

PREP + COOK TIME 40 MINUTES (+ REFRIGERATION) **SERVES** 4

2kg (4 pounds) american-style pork ribs

400g (12½ ounces) packaged shredded coleslaw mix

½ cup (125ml) coleslaw dressing

BARBECUE SAUCE

1 cup (250ml) tomato sauce (ketchup)

¾ cup (180ml) apple cider vinegar

2 tablespoons olive oil

¼ cup (60ml) worcestershire sauce

⅓ cup (75g) firmly packed brown sugar

2 tablespoons american mustard

1 teaspoon cracked black pepper

2 fresh small red thai (serrano) chillies, chopped finely

2 cloves garlic, crushed

2 tablespoons lemon juice

1 Make barbecue sauce.

2 Place ribs in a large shallow baking dish; pour barbecue sauce over ribs. Cover; refrigerate 3 hours or overnight, turning ribs occasionally.

3 Drain ribs; reserve sauce. Cook ribs on a heated oiled grill plate (or grill or barbecue), brushing occasionally with reserved sauce, for about 15 minutes or until cooked, turning ribs halfway through cooking time.

4 Bring any remaining sauce to the boil in a small saucepan; boil, uncovered, for about 5 minutes or until sauce thickens slightly.

5 Combine coleslaw and dressing in medium bowl.

6 Cut ribs into serving-sized pieces; serve with hot barbecue sauce and coleslaw.

BARBECUE SAUCE Bring ingredients to the boil in a medium saucepan. Cool for 10 minutes.

TIP Because it contains raw meat juices, the barbecue sauce used for marinating must be boiled for the time stated.

VEGETABLES

corn fritters with cucumber salad

PREP + COOK TIME 40 MINUTES SERVES 6

1 teaspoon ground cumin

½ teaspoon salt

375g (8 ounces) pancake shake mix

400g (12½ ounces) canned corn kernels, rinsed, drained

2 green onions (scallions), sliced thinly

2 tablespoons finely chopped fresh coriander (cilantro)

CUCUMBER SALAD

2 lebanese cucumbers (260g), sliced thinly

1 small red onion (100g), sliced thinly

1 fresh long red chilli, sliced thinly

⅓ cup loosely packed fresh coriander leaves (cilantro)

2 tablespoons sweet chilli sauce

1 tablespoon fish sauce

1 tablespoon lime juice

1 Add cumin and salt to pancake shake mix; return lid to jug, shake well to combine. Add water according to directions on container; return lid to jug, shake well. Pour into a medium-sized bowl. Add corn, onion and coriander; mix well.

2 Pour ¼ cup of the batter into a heated oiled large frying pan; using metal spatula, spread batter into round shape. Cook over medium heat, for 2 minutes each side or until fritter is cooked through. Remove fritter from pan; cover to keep warm. Repeat process, wiping out pan between batches and oiling if necessary, to make a total of 18 fritters.

3 Meanwhile, make cucumber salad. Serve fritters topped with salad.

CUCUMBER SALAD Combine cucumber, onion, chilli and coriander in a medium bowl. Combine remaining ingredients in a screw-top jar; shake well, drizzle over cucumber mixture.

nutritional count per serving

▶ 6.6g total fat
▶ 1.2g saturated fat
▶ 1367kJ (327 cal)
▶ 55.5g carbohydrate
▶ 9.7g protein
▶ 3.9g fibre

test kitchen tip

You can use 1½ cups (240g) of fresh or thawed frozen corn kernels instead of canned if you prefer.

This is a speedier vegetarian version of this Italian classic, which usually uses dried beans and ham hocks and requires long cooking times. You could use a can of red kidney beans if you can't find canned borlotti beans.

vegetable minestrone

PREP + COOK TIME 50 MINUTES **SERVES** 6

1 tablespoon olive oil

1 medium brown onion (150g), chopped coarsely

1 clove garlic, crushed

¼ cup (70g) tomato paste

1.5 litres (6 cups) water

2 cups (500ml) vegetable stock

2⅔ cups (700g) bottled tomato pasta sauce (passata)

1 celery stalk (150g), trimmed, chopped finely

1 medium carrot (120g), chopped finely

1 medium zucchini (120g), chopped finely

80g (2½ ounces) green beans, trimmed, sliced diagonally

400g (12½ ounces) canned borlotti beans, rinsed, drained

¾ cup (135g) macaroni

⅓ cup coarsely chopped fresh basil

1 Heat oil in a large saucepan; cook onion and garlic, stirring, until onion softens. Add paste; cook, stirring, for 2 minutes. Add the water, stock and pasta sauce; bring to the boil.

2 Add celery to pan; simmer, uncovered, for 10 minutes. Add carrot, zucchini and green beans; simmer, uncovered, for about 20 minutes or until carrot is tender. Add borlotti beans and pasta; simmer for about 10 minutes or until pasta is tender. Season to taste.

3 Serve soup topped with basil, and sprinkled with shaved parmesan, if you like.

test kitchen tip

For an even quicker version, use 2 cups frozen mixed diced vegetables instead of the fresh vegetables added in step 2.

nutritional count per serving

▸ 5.9g total fat

▸ 0.7g saturated fat

▸ 1046kJ (250 cal)

▸ 35.6g carbohydrate

▸ 9.4g protein

▸ 8.8g fibre

3 WAYS WITH PASSATA

chickpeas in spicy tomato sauce

PREP + COOK TIME 40 MINUTES SERVES 4

1 tablespoon olive oil

2 teaspoons cumin seeds

1 tablespoon ground coriander

¼ teaspoon cayenne pepper

1 medium brown onion (150g), chopped finely

2 cloves garlic, crushed

4 teaspoons grated fresh ginger

2 tablespoons tomato paste

2⅔ cups (700g) bottled tomato pasta sauce (passata)

1 cup (250ml) water

400g (12½ ounces) canned chickpeas (garbanzo beans)

10 baby carrots (200g), halved lengthways

750g (1½ pounds) canned tiny taters, rinsed, drained, quartered

½ cup coarsely chopped fresh coriander (cilantro)

1 Heat oil in a large saucepan; cook spices, stirring, until fragrant. Add onion, garlic and ginger; cook, stirring, until onion softens. Add tomato paste; cook, stirring, for 2 minutes.

2 Add sauce, the water and chickpeas to pan; bring to the boil. Reduce heat; simmer, uncovered, stirring occasionally, for 15 minutes or until mixture thickens slightly.

3 Add carrot and potato; cook, uncovered, for about 5 minutes or until carrot is tender and mixture has thickened. Remove from heat; stir in chopped coriander, season to taste.

nutritional count per serving
▶ 9.8g total fat
▶ 1.1g saturated fat
▶ 1406kJ (336 cal)
▶ 43.9g carbohydrate
▶ 11.9g protein
▶ 13.8g fibre

frying pan vegetable and ricotta lasagne

PREP + COOK TIME 50 MINUTES **SERVES** 6

1 tablespoon olive oil

1 large brown onion (200g), chopped finely

2 cloves garlic, crushed

1 x 250g (8-ounce) packet instant lasagne sheets (you need 11 sheets)

150g (4½ ounces) baby spinach leaves

500g (1 pound) antipasto vegetable mix

700g (1½-pounds) bottled tomato pasta sauce (passata)

1 cup (250ml) water

1½ cups (360g) firm ricotta, crumbled

1½ cups (150g) coarsely grated pizza cheese

1 Heat oil in a large deep frying pan; cook onion and garlic, stirring, until onion softens.

2 Meanwhile, break lasagne sheets lengthways into strips; put long strips aside, save any small broken pieces. Sprinkle small broken pasta pieces, spinach and antipasto into pan with onion; mix gently to combine.

3 Pour combined pasta sauce and the water into pan; insert long pasta strips into the mixture. Sprinkle with both cheeses. Bring the pan to the boil over high heat; reduce heat to low, cover, simmer, for 20 minutes.

4 Preheat grill (broiler).

5 Grill lasagne for 5 minutes or until cheese browns. Cover, stand for 5 minutes before serving.

3 WAYS WITH PASSATA

test kitchen tips

Use a large round deep frying pan, instead of a square one, with a base measurement of 28cm (11¼ inches) and a domed lid; cover the handle with aluminium foil to protect it from the heat of the grill. You could use a large flameproof baking dish (about 3-litres/12-cups) instead of the frying pan, if you prefer. Instead of breaking the pasta into long strips, simply break it all into bite-sized pieces; mix the pieces into the spinach and tomato sauce mixture, sprinkle over the cheese and cook the lasagne as directed.

nutritional count per serving
- ▶ 23g total fat
- ▶ 8g saturated fat
- ▶ 1980kJ (473 cal)
- ▶ 44g carbohydrate
- ▶ 21g protein
- ▶ 5g fibre

test kitchen tip

You need a deep frying pan measuring approximately 22cm (9 inches) across its base for this recipe; cover the handle with aluminium foil to protect it from the heat of the grill (broiler).

capsicum and potato frittata

PREP + COOK TIME 35 MINUTES SERVES 4

1 tablespoon olive oil

1 medium brown onion (150g), sliced thickly

⅓ cup (80g) drained roasted red capsicum (bell pepper) strips

750g (1½ pounds) canned tiny taters, rinsed, drained, sliced thickly

⅓ cup coarsely chopped fresh basil

¼ cup coarsely chopped fresh flat-leaf parsley

10 eggs, beaten lightly

½ cup (40g) coarsely grated parmesan

1 Heat oil in a large frying pan; cook onion, stirring, until softened. Stir in capsicum.

2 Layer potato evenly over capsicum in pan. Sprinkle herbs over potato layer then pour in egg. Cook, uncovered, over low heat, for about 8 minutes or until frittata starts to set around the edge of the pan.

3 Meanwhile, preheat grill (broiler).

4 Sprinkle frittata with parmesan; place pan under grill. Cook until frittata is set and browned lightly on top. Stand for 5 minutes before serving.

nutritional count per serving
- ▶ 22.5g total fat
- ▶ 6.9g saturated fat
- ▶ 1568kJ (375 cal)
- ▶ 17.7g carbohydrate
- ▶ 24.2g protein
- ▶ 3.2g fibre

lentil cottage pie

PREP + COOK TIME 1¾ HOURS **SERVES** 4

1 tablespoon olive oil

1 large brown onion (200g), chopped finely

1 medium red capsicum (bell pepper) (200g), chopped coarsely

2 medium zucchini (240g), chopped coarsely

1 medium eggplant (300g), chopped coarsely

2 cloves garlic, crushed

400g (12½ ounces) canned lentils, rinsed, drained

400g (12½ ounces) canned crushed tomatoes

4 green onions (scallions), chopped finely

600g (1¼-pound) tub prepared mashed potato

1 Preheat oven to 200°C/400°F.

2 Heat oil in a medium saucepan; cook brown onion, capsicum, zucchini, eggplant and garlic, stirring, until vegetables soften. Add lentils and tomato; bring to the boil. Reduce heat; simmer, uncovered, about 10 minutes or until mixture has thickened. Season to taste.

3 Meanwhile, stir green onion into mashed potato.

4 Spoon lentil mixture into an oiled shallow 2.5-litre (10-cup) baking dish; spread potato over top. Bake about 30 minutes or until top browns lightly.

nutritional count per serving
▶ 9.6g total fat
▶ 2.2g saturated fat
▶ 1192kJ (285 cal)
▶ 33.3g carbohydrate
▶ 10.7g protein
▶ 9.9g fibre

DESSERTS

pavlovas with crushed strawberries and cream

PREP + COOK TIME 10 MINUTES (+ STANDING) SERVES 4

250g (8 ounces) strawberries, coarsely chopped

1 tablespoon icing (confectioners') sugar

1 tablespoon orange-flavoured liqueur

300ml thickened (heavy) cream

4 pavlova nests

1 Combine strawberries, sugar and liqueur in a small bowl; crush lightly with a fork. Stand for 30 minutes.

2 Meanwhile, beat cream in a small bowl with an electric mixer until soft peaks form.

3 Place pavlovas on serving plates; top with strawberries and cream, dust with a little extra sifted icing sugar.

TIPS This dessert is our take on an Eton mess, a traditional English dessert consisting of a mixture of strawberries, meringue and cream. It was served at Eton College's annual cricket game. The strawberries should not be chopped too small or they will break down during standing. Pavlova nests are available from supermarkets.

nutritional count per serving
▶ 28.9g total fat
▶ 18.9g saturated fat
▶ 1396kJ (334 cal)
▶ 66.7g carbohydrate
▶ 6.3g protein
▶ 1.4g fibre

apple pie slice

PREP + COOK TIME 35 MINUTES (+ COOLING) **SERVES** 8

6 medium apples (900g), peeled, cored, cut into 1cm (½ inch) pieces

¼ cup (55g) caster (superfine) sugar

¼ cup (60ml) water

¾ cup (120g) sultanas

1 teaspoon mixed spice

2 teaspoons finely grated lemon rind

2 sheets shortcrust pastry

1 tablespoon milk

1 tablespoon caster (superfine) sugar, extra

1 Combine apple, sugar and the water in a large saucepan; cook, uncovered, stirring occasionally, for about 10 minutes or until apple softens. Remove from heat; stir in sultanas, spice and rind. Cool.

2 Preheat oven to 200°C/400°F. Grease a 20cm x 30cm (8-inch x 12-inch) lamington pan; line base with baking paper, extending paper 5cm (2 inches) over long sides of pan.

3 Place 1 pastry sheet over base of pan, trimming to fit. Spread apple filling over pastry. Top with remaining pastry; trim edges. Brush with milk; sprinkle with extra sugar. Bake about 25 minutes. Stand slice in pan for 5 minutes before cutting into eight slices.

SERVING SUGGESTION Serve warm apple pie slice with ice-cream or whipped cream. Ground nutmeg or cinnamon tastes great stirred through the ice-cream or cream.

nutritional count per slice
▶ 9.7g total fat
▶ 5.9g saturated fat
▶ 1463kJ (350 cal)
▶ 58.6g carbohydrate
▶ 4.8g protein
▶ 3.4g fibre

test kitchen tip

Make sure overhead exhaust fans are turned off before igniting the orange sauce. Be very careful when igniting the sauce – use extra long matches, available from supermarkets or camping stores. Igniting the sauce burns off the alcohol, leaving a more intense flavour. If you prefer, the sauce can be served as is, without first igniting it.

crêpes suzette

PREP + COOK TIME 15 MINUTES **SERVES** 4

125g (4 ounces) unsalted butter

½ cup (110g) caster (superfine) sugar

1½ cups (375ml) strained orange juice

2 tablespoons strained lemon juice

⅓ cup (80ml) orange-flavoured liqueur

8 frozen french-style crêpes (400g), thawed

2 medium oranges (480g), segmented

1 Melt butter in a large frying pan, add sugar; cook, stirring, until mixture begins to brown. Add juices; bring to the boil. Reduce heat; simmer, uncovered, for about 3 minutes or until golden. Remove from heat; add liqueur, ignite (see tip).

2 Fold crêpes in half then in half again, place in the sauce; warm over low heat.

3 Remove crêpes to serving plates; pour hot sauce over crêpes. Serve with orange segments.

nutritional count per serving
▶ 41g total fat
▶ 20.5g saturated fat
▶ 3039kJ (727 cal)
▶ 66.9g carbohydrate
▶ 10.3g protein
▶ 1.3g fibre

berry trifle

PREP + COOK TIME 15 MINUTES SERVES 6

300ml thickened (heavy) cream

2 teaspoons icing (confectioners') sugar

1 teaspoon vanilla extract

12 sponge finger biscuits (savoiardi) (180g)

1 cup (250ml) apple juice

1 cup (250ml) thick vanilla-flavoured custard

300g (9½ ounces) frozen mixed berries

1 Beat cream, sugar and extract in a small bowl with an electric mixer until soft peaks form.
2 Dip biscuits, one at a time, in juice; cover base of a 1.5-litre (6-cup) serving dish with some of the biscuits. Top with custard and half the berries. Top with remaining biscuits, cream and berries.

TIPS Use fresh berries if they are available. This trifle can also be layered with mango, banana and passionfruit pulp for a more tropical spin. Sponge finger biscuits are also known as savoiardi, savoy biscuits or lady's fingers; they are long, oval-shaped italian-style crisp fingers made from sponge-cake mixture. They are available from supermarkets.

nutritional count per serving
- ▶ 21.4g total fat
- ▶ 13.6g saturated fat
- ▶ 1434kJ (343 cal)
- ▶ 31.4g carbohydrate
- ▶ 5.7g protein
- ▶ 1.5g fibre

lamingtons

PREP TIME 30 MINUTES **MAKES** 24

4 cups (500g) icing (confectioner's) sugar

½ cup (50g) cocoa powder

20g (¾ ounce) butter, melted

⅔ cup (160ml) milk

450g (14½-ounce) store-bought packaged double rectangular sponge cake slabs

2½ cups (200g) desiccated coconut

1 Sift sugar and cocoa into a large heatproof bowl; stir in butter and milk. Stir icing over a large saucepan of simmering water until it is of a coating consistency.

2 Cut each slab into 12 squares. Dip squares in icing, drain off excess then toss in coconut; place lamingtons on a wire rack to set.

TIP We used a double rectangular slab sponge cake – these come in a pack of two sponges and are available from major supermarkets.

nutritional count per lamington

▶ 13.1g total fat ▶ 33.9g carbohydrate

▶ 9.1g saturated fat ▶ 3g protein

▶ 1120kJ (268 cal) ▶ 1.2g fibre

plum clafoutis

PREP + COOK TIME 45 MINUTES (+ COOLING) **SERVES** 6

⅔ cup (160ml) milk

⅔ cup (160ml) pouring cream

1 cinnamon stick

1 teaspoon vanilla extract

4 eggs

½ cup (110g) caster (superfine) sugar

¼ cup (35g) plain (all-purpose) flour

1kg (2 pounds) canned whole plums, drained, halved, seeded

1 Preheat oven to 200°C/400°F. Grease a shallow 2.5-litre (10-cup) ovenproof dish.

2 Combine milk, cream, cinnamon and extract in a medium saucepan; bring to the boil. Cool; remove cinnamon stick.

3 Whisk eggs and sugar in a medium bowl until light and frothy; whisk in flour, then whisk egg mixture into cream mixture.

4 Place plums in a shallow ovenproof dish; pour cream mixture over plums. Bake for about 30 minutes or until browned lightly.

5 Serve clafoutis dusted with sifted icing (confectioners') sugar and accompanied with cream or ice-cream, if you like.

nutritional count per serving
▶ 14.3g total fat
▶ 7.9g saturated fat
▶ 1394kJ (333 cal)
▶ 44.9g carbohydrate
▶ 7g protein
▶ 2.1g fibre

test kitchen tip

We used a low-calorie packet of jelly crystals because we wanted the cranberry and raspberry flavour but you can use any jelly crystals you like, as long as it makes 2 cups (500ml) jelly; raspberry, port wine or cherry-flavoured jelly would all work well.

raspberry jellies with sweet almond cream

PREP + COOK TIME 40 MINUTES (+ REFRIGERATION) **SERVES** 8

250g (8 ounces) fresh raspberries

90g (3 ounces) low-calorie cranberry and raspberry flavoured jelly crystals

2 tablespoons orange-flavoured liqueur

300ml thickened (heavy) cream

2 tablespoons icing (confectioner's) sugar

¾ cup (115g) vienna almonds, chopped coarsely

1 Wet the insides of eight ½-cup (125ml) moulds. Divide half the berries among moulds.

2 Make jelly according to directions on packet; stir in liqueur. Spoon two tablespoons of mixture over berries in each mould, cover; refrigerate for about 1 hour or until set. (Stand remaining mixture at room temperature.)

3 Pour remaining mixture carefully over set mixture in moulds, cover; refrigerate for about 3 hours, or overnight, until set.

4 Before serving, beat cream and sifted icing sugar in a small bowl with an electric mixer until soft peaks form. Fold in ½ cup nuts.

5 Wipe outsides of moulds with a hot cloth; turn jellies out onto serving plates. Serve with almond cream, sprinkled with remaining nuts and berries.

nutritional count per serving
▶ 20.1g total fat
▶ 9.9g saturated fat
▶ 1053kJ (252 cal)
▶ 12.6g carbohydrate
▶ 3.4g protein
▶ 2.8g fibre

lemon meringue cupcakes

PREP + COOK TIME 1 HOUR (+ COOLING) **MAKES** 12

You need a piping bag fitted with a 1cm (½-inch) plain piping tube.

470g (15-ounce) packet butter cake mix

1 cup (320g) lemon curd

COCONUT MERINGUE

4 egg whites

1 cup (220g) caster (superfine) sugar

1⅓ cups (95g) shredded coconut, chopped finely

nutritional count per cake
▶ 13.1g total fat
▶ (8.6g saturated fat)
▶ 1754kJ (419 cal)
▶ 69.7g carbohydrate
▶ 5.1g protein
▶ 1.2g fibre

1 Preheat oven to 180°C/350°F. Line a 12-hole standard (⅓-cup/80ml) muffin pan with paper cases.
2 Make cake according to directions on packet. Divide mixture into paper cases. Bake cakes about 20 minutes. Stand cakes in pan for 5 minutes before turning, top-side up, onto a wire rack to cool.
3 Increase oven temperature to 220°C/425°F.
4 Cut a deep hole into the centre of each cake (don't cut all the way through); discard cut pieces. Fill hole with curd.
5 Make coconut meringue. Spoon meringue into a piping bag fitted with a 1cm (½-inch) plain tube. Pipe meringue on top of each cake; place cakes on an oven tray.
6 Bake cakes for 5 minutes or until meringue is browned lightly.

COCONUT MERINGUE Beat egg whites in a small bowl with an electric mixer until soft peaks form; gradually add sugar, beating until sugar dissolves and mixture is thick and glossy. Fold in coconut.

bread and butter pudding

PREP + COOK TIME 1¼ HOURS SERVES 6

8 slices white bread (320g)

50g (1½ ounces) butter, softened

½ cup (80g) sultanas

1 litre (4 cups) thick custard

¼ teaspoon ground nutmeg

1 tablespoon icing (confectioners') sugar

1 Preheat oven to 160°C/325°F. Grease a shallow 2-litre (8-cup) ovenproof dish.

2 Discard crusts from bread. Spread each slice with butter; cut into four triangles. Layer bread, overlapping, in dish; sprinkle with sultanas. Pour custard over bread; sprinkle with nutmeg.

3 Bake pudding for about 50 minutes or until pudding is set (pudding will still have a slight wobble in centre). Stand pudding for 5 minutes; dust with sifted icing sugar to serve.

nutritional count per serving
- ▶ 13g total fat
- ▶ 8.2g saturated fat
- ▶ 1486kJ (355 cal)
- ▶ 51.2g carbohydrate
- ▶ 9.1g protein
- ▶ 4.5g fibre

apple and marmalade streusel puddings

PREP + COOK TIME 45 MINUTES (+ FREEZING) **SERVES** 4

800g (1½ pounds) canned pie apples

1 tablespoon caster (superfine) sugar

½ cup (170g) orange marmalade, warmed

STREUSEL

½ cup (75g) plain (all-purpose) flour

¼ cup (35g) self-raising flour

⅓ cup (75g) firmly packed brown sugar

½ teaspoon ground cinnamon

100g (3 ounces) butter, chopped

1 Make streusel.

2 Preheat oven to 200°C/400°F. Grease four 1-cup (250ml) ovenproof dishes.

3 Combine apple, sugar and warm marmalade in a medium bowl; divide apple mixture into dishes.

4 Coarsely grate streusel onto baking paper; sprinkle over apple mixture. Bake puddings for 20 minutes or until browned lightly.

STREUSEL Blend or process ingredients until combined. Roll into a ball; wrap in plastic. Freeze streusel for about 1 hour or until firm.

TIPS Streusel can be frozen for up to one week. Toss some frozen berries through the pie apple, if you like. Stewed rhubarb could be substituted for the canned pie apples.

nutritional count per serving

▶ 21g total fat   ▶ 92.4g carbohydrate

▶ 13.6g saturated fat   ▶ 3.6g protein

▶ 2378kJ (568 cal)   ▶ 4.5g fibre

COOKING TECHNIQUES

Trimming watercress This peppery green is grown in water; use scissors to cut off the roots then pull the leaves off any thick, woody stems.

Preparing asparagus To snap the woody end off the asparagus, hold it close to the base and bend it until it snaps. Discard the woody end. Trim with a vegetable peeler.

Trimming beetroot Cut the stems to 2cm (¾ inch) of the bulb, and don't trim the beard at the base of the plant; this stops the colour from bleeding during cooking.

To grate beetroot, use the coarse (large) holes of the grater. It's best to wear disposable gloves as the juice will stain your hands.

To remove corn from fresh cobs, remove the husk (the outer covering) and the silk (the soft silky inner threads), and trim one side of the corn cob so it lies flat. Use a large flat-bladed knife to cut down the cob, close to the core, to remove the kernels.

Grating lime Use the small holes on a grater to finely grate the lime rind, ensuring that only the rind is grated, and not the bitter white pith underneath. Rasp graters (thin metal graters), such as a Microplane grater, can also be used.

Crushing garlic Press unpeeled garlic firmly with the flat blade of a large knife (top) crushing the clove. Pull off the papery skin and chop the clove finely with the knife. A garlic press (bottom) removes and leaves the skin behind while crushing the garlic.

To use fresh thyme leaves, hold the top of the stem with one hand and run the fingers of the other hand down the stem to strip off the leaves. Any small, thin stems that break away with the leaves are fine to use.

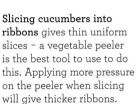

Slicing cucumbers into ribbons gives thin uniform slices – a vegetable peeler is the best tool to use to do this. Applying more pressure on the peeler when slicing will give thicker ribbons.

Zesting citrus fruit A zester has very small, and very sharp, holes that cut the rind (the outermost layer of the fruit) into thin ribbons but leaves the bitter pith behind.

To slice a capsicum, cut the top and bottom off and stand it on one end; slice down removing all the flesh. Remove and discard the seeds and membranes, and slice the flesh.

Chiffonade is a way of cutting green leaves into long, thin strips. Lay leaves flat on top of each other, then roll up tightly and cut into thin slices.

Pitting an olive is easy with on olive pitter, pictured; just put the olive in the cup and push, and out pops the seed. To do this by hand, crush the olive with the flat side of a large knife and slip the seed out. The olives will then be easy to chop.

To shell a prawn, hold the body with one hand, twist the head with the other and pull it away from the body. Roll the shell off from the underside with the legs still attached. If removing the tail, squeeze the tail on both sides to release the shell from the flesh and remove.

Cutting an onion into wedges Cut the onion in half lengthways through the root. Remove the papery outer skin. Lie the onion cut-side down and cut the onion lengthways through the root into triangular-shaped wedges. The root holds the wedges together.

Hull a strawberry The hull, or calyx, is the green leafy top. Wash and gently pat the strawberries dry, then cut around the leafy top and into the pale flesh underneath (you may find it easier to pull the leaves off before cutting into the strawberry.

GLOSSARY

AMERICAN-STYLE PORK SPARE RIBS
usually sold in long slabs or racks of 10
to 12 ribs, trimmed so little fat remains;
are the ones to slather with barbecue
sauce and cook on the barbie.

BACON
shortcut is a 'half rasher'; the streaky
(belly), narrow portion of the rasher has
been removed leaving the choice cut eye
meat (fat end).
streaky from the belly of the pig. Comes
in strips with long veins of fat running
parallel to the rind.

BAKING PAPER also parchment paper
or baking parchment – a silicone-coated
paper primarily used for lining baking
pans and oven trays so biscuits and cakes
won't stick, making removal easy.

BEANS
borlotti also known as roman beans or
pink beans. They are interchangeable
with pinto beans because of the
similarity in appearance – both are pale
pink or beige with dark red streaks.
broad also known as fava, windsor and
horse beans; available dried, fresh, canned
and frozen. Fresh and frozen beans
should be peeled twice (discarding both
the outer long green pod and the beige-
green tough inner shell) before using.
kidney medium-sized red bean, slightly
floury in texture yet sweet in flavour;
it's found in bean mixes and is the bean
used in chilli con carne.
snake long (about 40cm/16 inches),
thin, fresh green beans; Asian in origin,
with a taste similar to green or french
beans. Used most frequently in stir-fries,
they are also known as yard-long beans
because of their (pre-metric) length.
sprouts also known as bean shoots;
tender new growths of assorted beans
and seeds germinated for consumption
as sprouts. The most readily available
are alfalfa, mung beans, soya beans and
snow pea sprouts.
white in this book, some recipes may
simply call for 'white beans', a generic
term we use for canned or dried haricot,
cannellini, navy or great northern beans
(all can be substituted for the other).

BICARBONATE OF SODA also known
as baking or carb soda; used as a
leavening agent in baking.

BREAD
ciabatta in Italian, the word means
'slipper', the traditional shape of this
popular white bread with a crisp crust.
french also known as french stick,
french loaf or baguette. Bread that's
formed into a long, narrow cylindrical
loaf. It usually has a crisp brown crust
and light chewy interior.
pitta also known as lebanese bread. A
wheat-flour pocket bread sold in large,
flat pieces that separate into two thin
rounds. Also available in small thick
pieces called pocket pitta.
tortillas thin, round unleavened bread;
two kinds are available, one made from
wheat flour and the other from corn.

BUTTER use salted or unsalted (sweet)
butter; 125g is equal to one stick (4oz)
of butter.

BUTTERMILK originally the term given
to the slightly sour liquid left after
butter was churned from cream, today
it is made similarly to yoghurt. Despite
the implication of its name, it is low in
fat. Sold alongside fresh milk products
in supermarkets.

CAPERS the grey-green buds of a warm
climate (usually Mediterranean) shrub,
sold either dried and salted or pickled in
a vinegar brine. Tiny young ones, called
baby capers, are also available both in
brine or dried in salt. Capers, whether
packed in brine or in salt, must be rinsed
well before using.

CAPSICUM also known as bell pepper
or pepper. Native to Central and South
America; found in red, green, yellow,
orange or purplish-black varieties. Seeds
and membranes should be discarded
before use.

CHEESE
cheddar a semi-hard cows'-milk cheese.
It ranges in colour from white to pale
yellow, and has a slightly crumbly texture
if properly matured. The flavour becomes
sharper with time.
fetta a salty, white cheese with a milky,
fresh acidity. Most commonly made
from cows' milk, although sheep and
goat varieties are also available.
gruyère a swiss cheese having small
holes and a nutty, slightly salty flavour.
haloumi a firm, cream-coloured sheep-
milk cheese matured in brine; somewhat
like a minty, salty fetta in flavour. It can
be grilled or fried, briefly, but must be
eaten as soon as possible after cooking
as it becomes rubbery on standing.
mascarpone a fresh, unripened, creamy,
triple cream cheese with a rich, slightly
tangy taste and a creamy yellow colour.
mozzarella a soft, spun-curd cheese. It
has a low melting point and wonderfully
elastic texture when heated; is used to
add texture rather than flavour.
parmesan also known as parmigiano;
a hard, grainy, cows'-milk cheese. The
curd is salted in brine for a month
before being aged for up to two years
in humid conditions.
pizza a blend of grated mozzarella,
cheddar and parmesan cheeses.
provolone a mild cheese when young,
similar to mozzarella. Golden yellow in
colour, with a smooth shiny skin.
ricotta is a sweet, white, moist cows'-
milk cheese; the name roughly translates
as 'cooked again'. It's made from whey,
a by-product of other cheese-making, to
which fresh milk and acid are added.

CHICKPEAS also called garbanzos,
channa or hummus; an irregularly
round, sandy-coloured legume.

CHILLI available in many different types
and sizes (usually the smaller the chilli
the hotter it is). Use rubber gloves when
seeding and chopping fresh chillies as
they can burn your skin. Removing seeds
and membranes lessens the heat level.
chilli jam a sweet, sourish tangy jam
that is sold in jars at supermarkets and
Asian food stores. Used in stir-fries,
sauces and some soups. After opening,
store it in the refrigerator.
green any unripened chilli; also some
particular varieties that are ripe when
green, such as jalapeño and habanero.
long available both fresh and dried; a
generic term used for any moderately
hot, long (about 6cm-8cm), thin chilli.
thai red also known as 'scuds'; tiny,
very hot and bright red in colour.

COCONUT
desiccated unsweetened, concentrated,
dried, finely shredded coconut.
shredded thin strips of dried coconut.

CORIANDER also known as pak chee,
cilantro or chinese parsley; bright-green
leafy herb with a pungent flavour. Both
the stems and roots are used in cooking;
wash well before using. Don't substitute
coriander seeds or powder (ground) for
fresh as the tastes are very different.

COUSCOUS a fine, grain-like cereal
product made from semolina; it is
rehydrated by steaming, or with the
addition of a warm liquid, and swells
to three or four times its original size.

CREAM we used fresh cream also known as pouring, pure and single cream, unless otherwise stated. It has no additives unlike commercially thickened cream. Minimum fat content 35%.
sour a thick commercially-cultured soured cream. Minimum fat content 35%.
thickened a single cream containing a thickening agent; is used for whipping. Minimum fat content 35%.

CRISPY FRIED NOODLES are sold packaged (commonly a 100g/3oz) packet), already deep-fried and ready to eat. They are sometimes labelled crunchy noodles, and are available in two widths – thin and spaghetti-like or wide and flat like fettuccine.

DILL PICKLE a very small variety of pickled cucumber that, when pickled with dill, is known as a dill pickle.

FILLO PASTRY also known as filo or phyllo; tissue-thin pastry sheets purchased chilled or frozen.

FLOUR
plain (all-purpose) made from wheat; has no raising agent.
self-raising (rising) plain flour sifted with baking powder in the proportion of 1 cup flour to 2 teaspoons baking powder.

GARAM MASALA a blend of spices based on varying proportions of cardamom, cloves, cinnamon, coriander, fennel and cumin, roasted and ground together. Black pepper and chilli can be added for a hotter version.

GRAPE TOMATO named as it is about the size of a grape; they can be oblong, pear or grape-shaped and are often used whole in salads or eaten as a snack.

GREEN CURRY PASTE is the hottest of the traditional pastes; it contains chilli, garlic, onion, lemon grass, galangal and other spices.

KITCHEN STRING made of a natural product such as cotton or hemp, so that it neither affects the flavour of the food it's tied around nor melts when heated.

LAKSA CURRY PASTE includes chillies, lemon grass, galangal, shrimp paste, onions and turmeric. Commercial laksa pastes vary dramatically in their heat intensity, so use less of the laksa paste you've purchased until you can determine how hot it makes the final dish.

LAMINGTON PAN 20cm x 30cm slab cake pan, 3cm deep (8in x 12in x 1¼in).

LEBANESE CUCUMBER short, slender and thin-skinned. Probably the most popular variety because of its tender, edible skin, tiny, yielding seeds and sweet, fresh and flavoursome taste.

LEMON GRASS a tall, clumping, lemon-smelling and -tasting, sharp-edged grass; only the white lower part of each stem is used in cooking. Bruise the lemon grass by hitting the lower white bulb with the flat side of a heavy knife or cleaver – this helps to release its flavour and aroma.

LETTUCE, BUTTER also known as boston lettuce. Has small, round, loosely formed heads with a sweet flavour; soft, buttery-textured leaves range from pale green on the outer leaves to pale yellow-green inner leaves.

MESCLUN pronounced mess-kluhn; also known as mixed greens, spring salad mix or baby salad mix. A blend of assorted young lettuce and other green leaves, including baby spinach leaves, mizuna and curly endive.

MIZUNA Japanese in origin; a feathery green salad leaf having a sharp, slightly mustardy, flavour.

MUSHROOMS
button small, cultivated white mushrooms with a mild flavour. If a recipe calls for an unspecified mushroom, use button.
flat large, flat mushrooms with a rich earthy flavour, ideal for filling and barbecuing. They are sometimes misnamed field mushrooms, which are wild mushrooms.
oyster also known as abalone; a grey-white mushroom shaped like a fan. Prized for its smooth texture and subtle, oyster-like flavour.
shiitake when fresh are known as chinese black, forest or golden oak mushrooms; although cultivated they have the earthiness and taste of wild mushrooms. Are large and meaty. When dried, they are known as donko or dried chinese mushrooms; rehydrate before use.
swiss brown also known as cremini or roman mushrooms, are light brown mushrooms having a full-bodied flavour. Button or cup mushrooms can be substituted. The large variety are often known as portobello mushrooms.

MUSTARD
american-style a sweet-tasting mustard containing mustard seeds, sugar, salt, spices and garlic.

dijon a pale brown, distinctively flavoured, fairly mild french mustard.
wholegrain also known as seeded mustard. A french-style coarse-grain mustard made from crushed mustard seeds and dijon-style french mustard.

OCEAN TROUT a farmed fish with pink, soft flesh. It is from the same family as the atlantic salmon; one can be substituted for the other. Available fresh or smoked.

OIL
cooking spray we use a cholesterol-free cooking spray made from canola oil.
olive made from ripened olives. Extra virgin and virgin are the best, while extra light or light refers to taste not fat levels.
peanut pressed from ground peanuts; most commonly used oil in Asian cooking as it has a high smoke point (capacity to handle high heat without burning).
sesame made from roasted, crushed, white sesame seeds; a flavouring rather than a cooking medium.
vegetable sourced from plants rather than animal fats.

PAPRIKA ground dried sweet red capsicum (bell pepper); there are many grades and types available including sweet, hot, mild and smoked.

PAVLOVA NESTS small crisp meringue nests available from supermarkets.

POLENTA also known as cornmeal; a flour-like cereal made of dried corn (maize) and sold ground in different textures. Also the name of the dish made from it.

PREPARED HORSERADISH preserved grated horseradish root.

RED CURRY PASTE a hot blend of dried red chillies, onions, garlic, lemon rind, oil, shrimp paste, ground cumin, paprika, turmeric and black pepper.

RICE
basmati a white, fragrant long-grained rice. Wash several times before cooking.
calrose an extremely versatile medium-grain rice; can be substituted for short- or long-grain rices if necessary.
jasmine fragrant long-grained rice; white rice, either long- or short-grain, can be substituted, but will not taste the same.
long-grain elongated grains that remain separate when cooked; this is the most popular steaming rice in Asia.

ROCKET also known as arugula, rugula and rucola; a peppery green leaf. Baby rocket is smaller and less peppery.

SAUCES

fish also called nam pla or nuoc nam; made from pulverised salted fermented fish, most often anchovies. Has a pungent smell and strong taste, so use sparingly.

hoisin a thick, sweet and spicy chinese paste made from salted fermented soya beans, onions and garlic.

satay the traditional Indonesian/Malaysian spicy peanut sauce served with grilled meat skewers.

soy made from fermented soya beans. Several variations are available in most supermarkets and Asian food stores.

japanese soy an all-purpose low-sodium soy sauce made with more wheat content than its Chinese counterparts; fermented in barrels and aged. Possibly the best table soy, and the one to choose if you only want one variety.

kecap asin a thick, salty dark soy sauce.

kecap manis a dark, thick, sweet soy sauce used in most South-East Asian cuisines. Depending on the brand, the soy's sweetness is derived from the addition of either molasses or palm sugar when brewed.

light soy a fairly thin, pale and salty soy sauce; used in dishes in which the natural colour of the ingredients is to be maintained. Not to be confused with salt-reduced or low-sodium soy sauces.

sweet chilli a comparatively mild, thai-style sauce made from red chillies, garlic, sugar and vinegar.

Tabasco brand name of an extremely fiery sauce made from vinegar, thai red chillies and salt.

worcestershire a thin, dark-coloured sauce made from garlic, lime, soy sauce, tamarind, onions, molasses, anchovies, vinegar and other seasonings.

SPICES

allspice also known as pimento or jamaican pepper; so-named because it tastes like a combination of nutmeg, cumin, clove and cinnamon – all spices.

cardamom native to India and used extensively in its cuisine; purchased in pod, seed or ground form. Has a aromatic, sweetly rich flavour. Is one of the world's most expensive spices.

chinese five-spice a fragrant mixture of ground cinnamon, cloves, star anise, sichuan pepper and fennel seeds.

cinnamon the ground inner bark of the shoots of the cinnamon tree; also available in stick (quill) form.

cloves dried flower buds of a tropical tree; can be used whole or in ground form. Has a distinctively pungent and 'spicy' scent and flavour.

cumin a spice also known as zeera or comino; has a spicy, nutty flavour.

ginger also known as powdered ginger; used as a flavouring in cakes, pies and puddings but cannot be substituted for fresh ginger.

mixed spice a classic mixture generally containing caraway, allspice, coriander, cumin, nutmeg and ginger, although cinnamon and other spices can be added.

ras el hanout a classic spice blend used in Moroccan cooking. The name means 'top of the shop' or the very best spice blend that a spice merchant has to offer. Most versions contain over a dozen spices, including cardamom, mace, nutmeg, cinnamon, and ground chilli.

sumac a purple-red, astringent spice ground from the berries that grow on shrubs flourishing wild around the Mediterranean; adds a tart, lemony flavour to food.

SPLIT PEAS a variety of yellow or green pea grown specifically for drying. When dried, the peas usually split along a natural seam. Whole and split dried peas are available in supermarkets and health-food stores.

SPONGE FINGER BISCUITS are also known as savoiardi, savoy biscuits or lady's fingers; they are long, oval-shaped italian-style crisp fingers made from sponge-cake mixture. They are available from supermarkets.

SUGAR

brown a finely granulated, extremely soft sugar retaining molasses for its characteristic colour and flavour.

caster also known as superfine or finely granulated table sugar.

icing sugar also known as confectioners' or powdered sugar; granulated sugar crushed together with a small amount of cornflour added to stop clumping.

palm sugar also known as nam tan pip, jaggery, jawa or gula melaka; made from the sap of the sugar palm tree. Light brown to black in colour and usually sold in rock-hard cakes; if unavailable, substitute it with brown sugar.

raw natural brown granulated sugar.

white a coarse, granulated table sugar, also known as crystal sugar.

SULTANAS dried grapes, also known as golden raisins.

TACO SEASONING MIX found in most supermarkets; is meant to duplicate the taste of a Mexican sauce made from oregano, cumin, chillies and other spices.

TZATZIKI a Greek yoghurt dip made with cucumber, garlic and sometimes chopped fresh mint.

VANILLA

bean a dried, long, thin pod from a tropical orchid; the minuscule black seeds imparts a luscious vanilla flavour. Split the bean in half lengthwise using a small sharp knife. Hold the pod at one end and then scrape the seeds free from both sides of the bean with the edge of the knife or a teaspoon.

extract made by extracting the flavour from the vanilla bean pod; the pods are soaked, usually in alcohol, to capture the authentic flavour.

VINEGAR

apple cider made from fermented apples.

balsamic made from the juice of Trebbiano grapes; is a deep rich brown colour with a sweet and sour flavour; there are now many balsamic vinegars on the market ranging in pungency and quality depending on how long they have been aged. Quality can be determined up to a point by price; use the most expensive sparingly.

red wine based on fermented red wine.

rice a colourless vinegar made from fermented rice and flavoured with sugar and salt. Also known as seasoned rice vinegar; sherry can be substituted.

white made from spirit of cane sugar.

white wine made from white wine.

WATER CHESTNUT resembles a chestnut in appearance, hence the English name. They are small brown tubers with a crisp, white, nutty-tasting flesh. Their crunchy texture is best experienced fresh, however, canned water chestnuts are more easily obtained and can be kept about a month, once opened, under refrigeration.

ZUCCHINI also known as courgette; small, pale- or dark-green, yellow or white vegetable belonging to the squash family. Harvested when young, its edible flowers can be stuffed then deep-fried or oven-baked to make a delicious appetiser.

INDEX

Published in 2014 by Bauer Media Books

Bauer Media Books is a division of Bauer Media Limited

54 Park St, Sydney

GPO Box 4088, Sydney, NSW 2001.

phone (02) 9282 8618; fax (02) 9126 3702

www.awwcookbooks.com.au

MEDIA GROUP

BAUER MEDIA BOOKS

Publisher - Sally Wright

Editorial and Food Director - Pamela Clark

Sales & rights director Brian Cearnes

Creative Director - Hieu Chi Nguyen

Published and Distributed in the United Kingdom by Octopus Publishing Group

Endeavour House

189 Shaftesbury Avenue

London WC2H 8JY

United Kingdom

phone (+44)(0)207 632 5400; fax (+44)(0)207 632 5405

info@octopus-publishing.co.uk;

www.octopusbooks.co.uk

Printed by Toppan Printing Co., China

International foreign language rights, Brian Cearnes, Bauer Media Books bcearnes@bauer-media.com.au

A catalogue record for this book is available from the British Library.

ISBN: 978 1 909770 06 5 (pbk.)

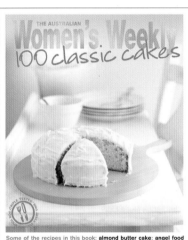

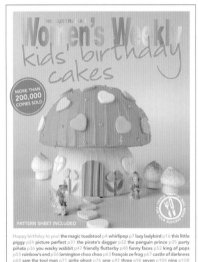
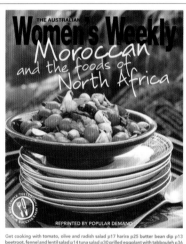